THE MAGIC
ORPHIC HYMNS

"This book is a marvel of pagan revivalism. Tamra Lucid and Ronnie Pontiac have created a symphonic and learned study of the Orphic mythos encompassing history and meaning; translation of key odes; and reconstructed practice. If you yearn for evidence that the old deities are with us today, look no further than *The Magic of the Orphic Hymns*."

MITCH HOROWITZ, PEN AWARD–WINNING AUTHOR OF
OCCULT AMERICA AND *UNCERTAIN PLACES*

"This fascinating, lively, and erudite exploration of Orphism is a superb entrance point to this treasure trove of lore and knowledge."

RICHARD SMOLEY, EDITOR OF *QUEST: JOURNAL OF
THE THEOSOPHICAL SOCIETY IN AMERICA* AND
AUTHOR OF *A THEOLOGY OF LOVE*

"Tamra Lucid and Ronnie Pontiac have produced a beautifully clear and elegant version of the ancient Orphic hymns, preceded by a meticulously researched mythic, historical, and magical overview of all things Orphic past and present. They are passionate and thorough, their tone contemporary and accessible, creating a wonderful example of what Jeff Kripal calls 'the gnostic classroom,' which is rigorously scholarly yet deeply sympathetic to the universal wisdom of the Orphic tradition. A great resource for students and practitioners alike."

ANGELA VOSS, EDITOR OF *MARSILIO FICINO*
(WESTERN ESOTERIC MASTERS SERIES)

"A wonderful book for anyone interested in metaphysics and mythology. Not only a fascinating and easy-to-read history but also an exhaustive work of scholarship—and in the translations of the poems that make up the second half of the book, a mind-blowing work of creativity. A must for any visionary's library."

TOD DAVIES, AUTHOR OF THE HISTORY OF ARCADIA
VISIONARY FICTION SERIES AND EDITORIAL DIRECTOR
OF EXTERMINATING ANGEL PRESS

"The Orphic hymns are among the most beautiful and effective invocations that have been handed down to us from the ancient Greeks. But, while Taylor's classic translations are both admirable and eloquent in practice—that is, used ritualistically—they can seem clumsy and, at times, even cumbersome. Pontiac and Lucid's welcome interpretive renditions have changed all of that. Theirs have quickly become my go-to translations for using the hymns in practical theurgic rites."

P. D. NEWMAN AUTHOR OF
THEURGY: THEORY AND PRACTICE

"Ronnie Pontiac and Tamra Lucid, musicians and metaphysicians both, the inheritors of Manly P. Hall's blessings. Who better to reveal the living magic of the Orphic hymns to a new generation? The Orphic hymns are not spells but poetic and magical evocations aligned with the understanding of pantheism, that all of nature is divinely infused and revealed through its kindred correspondences. Although the book chases the figure of Orpheus through history in a scholarly fashion, the author is not identified, the story is too complex and veiled. The magic is to be encountered in the song, not the singer, so take up the invitation and softly sing to the world outside your window."

NAOMI OZANIEC,
AUTHOR OF *BECOMING A GARMENT OF ISIS*

"This book delivers what its title indicates: the translations of the Orphic fragments and hymns are rendered in clear modern English, easy to understand for the contemporary reader. The review and analysis of scholarship on the contested 'Orphic' religion is wide ranging and comprehensive. All scholarship is taken into consideration from skeptical classicists to engaged occultists. The book presents a 'feeling' of the Orphic tradition and at the same time an analytic and critical overview of 'Orphism' from ancient to modern times. From the ancient poets to the modern painters of Orphism; from Plato and Plotinus to Ficino, Thomas Taylor, and E. R. Dodds; from Monteverdi to Philip Glass to modern pop culture—it is an accomplishment. I give my warmest endorsement."

JAY BREGMAN, AUTHOR OF *SYNESIUS OF CYRENE*

THE MAGIC OF THE
ORPHIC HYMNS

A New Translation
for the Modern Mystic

Tamra Lucid & Ronnie Pontiac

Inner Traditions
Rochester, Vermont

Inner Traditions
One Park Street
Rochester, Vermont 05767
www.InnerTraditions.com

Text stock is SFI certified

Cataloging-in-Publication Data for this title is available from the Library of Congress

ISBN 978-1-64411-720-0 (print)
ISBN 978-1-64411-721-7 (ebook)

Printed and bound in the United States by Lake Book Manufacturing, LLC
The text stock is SFI certified. The Sustainable Forestry Initiative® program
promotes sustainable forest management.

10 9 8 7 6 5 4 3 2 1

Text design and layout by Priscilla Harris Baker
This book was typeset in Garamond Premier Pro with Alchemist, Fritz
Quadrata, and Hypatia Sans used as display typefaces

To send correspondence to the author of this book, mail a first-class letter
to the author c/o Inner Traditions • Bear & Company, One Park Street,
Rochester, VT 05767, and we will forward the communication.

Dedicated to Manly Palmer Hall

ACKNOWLEDGMENTS

We thank Tod Davies, Jay Bregman, Apostolos Athanassakis, Norman Arthur Johnson, Nicholas LaCerf, Angela Voss, P. D. Newman, Normandi Ellis, Kimberly Cooper Nichols, Randy Roark, Sasha Chaitow, David Fideler, Kenneth Atchity, and Jon Graham.

I learned from Orpheus that love existed, and that it held the keys to the whole world, the whole power of magic consists in love.

MARSILIO FICINO

Orphism was the product of Pythagorean influence on Bacchic mysteries.

JAN BREMMER

Orpheus playing a vihuela. Frontispiece of the vihuela tablature book by Luis De Milán, *Libro de música de vihuela de mano intitulado El maestro* (1536).

Contents

Orphic Charms and the Sacred Songs of Orpheus

Orphic Charms–120
Messages on gold leaf buried with the dead,
and a grand invocation.

The Sacred Songs of Orpheus–134
A poetic interpretation of the Orphic hymns with added
details about the sacred correspondences of the gods.

An Experiment with the Orphic Hymns

Many consider Marsilio Ficino the father of the Renaissance. He was a Catholic priest but he wrote: "no magic is more powerful than that of the Orphic hymns." As we shall see in chapter 8, he not only sang them in rituals and for his friends, he also translated them into a language they could understand.

What is a magical formula exactly? If the definition is a ritual to bend the world to our will for the attainment of a goal, the hymns would not qualify. But they do if we define a magical formula as a rite of purification, or a way of lifting the soul to be healed or improved by contact with the divine, a tuning to the higher order of nature, a deeper realignment with life.

Long before this book was written, our limited but intriguing experience with the hymns began when we—Ronnie Pontiac and Tamra Lucid—worked with Manly Palmer Hall in the 1980s. Hall's Philosophical Research Society republished Thomas Taylor's influential eighteenth-century translation, titled *The Mystical Hymns of Orpheus*, which had been an inspiration to great writers like William Blake and Ralph Waldo Emerson. Ronnie was one of several people at the Philosophical Research Society who helped to prepare the reprint for publication. The hymns of Orpheus fascinated us but we found the antiquated translation frustrating. Around the same time, while a student in college, Ronnie studied ancient Greek. He borrowed the ponderous *Liddell and Scott's Greek-English Lexicon* to work out the individual words of the hymns. Meanwhile, Tamra researched her half of our shared library for herbs, scents, times of day, and other correspondences associated with specific gods. Once Ronnie had a translation of every word in the hymns, and Tamra had the corresponding elements, we created these poetic interpretations.

We wanted some idea of how the hymns worked. What was Ficino talking about when he referred to their magical power? The plan was to softly sing each hymn at our window to the outside world, usually but not necessarily at dawn or dusk. The window overlooked a street of apartment buildings, but we could see a few trees and the sky above. Where possible they would be performed on days that traditionally corresponded to celebrations of the deity.

We decided if we were going to try the hymns out, we should be drug and alcohol free. We also followed the Orphic diet as closely as we were able, avoiding meat and beans among other traditionally impure foods.

Our experiences were serendipitous, to say the least. An owl landed on a telephone pole across the street during the hymn to owl-eyed Athena. When it took flight it swooped directly toward us. A couple walking together paused under the window to share a kiss during the hymn to Aphrodite. In an otherwise blue sky, thunder rumbled and lightning flashed at the moment the hymn to thundering Zeus ended. Winds blew from the west during the hymn to the west wind, and the same for the other directions.

We continued to insist these must be coincidences. Looking ahead several days to a hymn that mentioned rain, we checked the weather forecast: sunny skies; not surprising in Southern California. But local news anchors buzzed about the "surprise shower" that day.

We didn't know what to make of it. We didn't believe that we were creating the phenomena. It felt more like being pulled into harmony with a series of improbable events. We felt more like witnesses than active agents.

Several years later, we read about Ficino's similar experiences and his recommendation that "no magic is more powerful than that of the Orphic hymns." We don't expect anyone to believe it. We wouldn't have believed it ourselves, or our senses, if we hadn't both been there.

We didn't try to replicate the results. We thought innocence can only be as good as wisdom on rare occasions, and not everyone is so lucky their first time. We quietly continued our research while pursuing other activities.

In 2020, while on lockdown in Los Angeles during the pandemic, we encountered a quote by the founder of Shingon Buddhism, Kōbō Daishi. At the end of his *The Secret Key to the Heart Sutra* he wrote:

> It is the year 818 and a great epidemic is sweeping the country. The Emperor personally copied the Heart Sutra with a brush dipped in gold ink. Following the pattern of other commentaries, I have composed a work on the main points of the sutra, and even before I uttered the words marking the end of this task, people who recovered from their illness were standing about the roadways. Night had turned into the brilliant light of day. (Dreitlein 2011)

3

We thought of the hymns of Orpheus and decided we would use them for a humble imitation of the emperor's ritual. We viewed the hymns as poetic sigils and worked together to carefully craft every line.

On the night we finished the first final draft, male howling and female screams erupted just west of us in the canyon. Like the cries of the satyrs and maenads, these echoing voices carried an uncanny undertone of terror. We've lived in the canyon for twenty years and have heard all manner of cries, but nothing like this.

The location of the cries happened to be a place once described to us by a late neighbor. She reminisced about being a teenager in 1967 during the Summer of Love when there were few houses in the canyon. She and her friends would take a dirt trail down to Sunset Boulevard where they saw Jimi Hendrix play the Whiskey. She said there had been a certain palm tree they would gather under to share wine and read poetry aloud. They called themselves the Dionysus Society.

The Mythology of Orpheus

Vegetarian, nonviolent, a singer and string strummer, a poet, a broken-hearted lover, a traveler to other worlds, not just on the first tour bus in Western history, a ship called the *Argo,* but also beyond death, to the world of gods and ghosts. Haters snickered that he was effeminate and probably gay. But his fans say all the wisdom in the world is in his songs. If you know how to listen, if you get the music, if you understand the symbolism of the lyrics, all the secrets of life and death are revealed.

As befits the first rock star in history, frenzied women tore Orpheus apart. He suffered what the record company always feared would happen to the Beatles if their screaming fans ever caught up with them. His body parts thrown in the river, the head of Orpheus went on singing, like the hit singles of dead teen idols and the touring hologram of Roy Orbison, the midcentury American pop singer of songs of lost love.

It would not be an overstatement to describe Orphic literature as the grow light for Western cultural renaissance. Wherever Orpheus descended into the underground of composers, painters, musicians, philosophers, and mystics, a flowering of culture followed, and the arts flourished.

For generations historians believed that Western civilization began in ancient Greece. Today, historians have the evidence to support the testimony of the ancient Greeks themselves that other cultures, especially the ancient Egyptian, gave Greece important inspiration and key ideas about the esoteric.

But thanks to the works of Plato and Aristotle, the comedies of Aristophanes, and the tragedies of Aeschylus, in many ways we can still view ancient Greece as the flashpoint where the inferno that is the Western world began. As we shall see, we can also look to Greece for what may be the earliest recognizable counterculture in Western history.

The ancient Greeks believed that Orpheus lived just one generation before the siege of Troy. But the name Orpheus first appears more than six hundred years after, in a fragment from the sixth century BCE by the poet Ibykus: "famous Orpheus." Homer and Hesiod never mention him, but Pindar (ca. 500 BCE) calls him "father of songs." Aristotle denied there ever was a real Orpheus. Some scholars have offered a list of five men by that name, none any more substantial than the mythic Orpheus.

What can the famous name tell us? The -eus ending is commonly associated with ancient Greece before Homer. Historian Martin Bernal suggests Orpheus derives from orpais, the ancient Greek transcription of the ancient Egyptian word for "hereditary prince." Bernal believes Orpheus is how the Greeks interpreted the ancient Egyptian earth god Geb, though the two don't seem to have that much in common in the myths that survive to us.

With the dubious certainty of late nineteenth-century occult scholarship, Helena P. Blavatsky declared that Orpheus was Hindu, likewise the god Dionysus. Orpheus, she believed, brought the hymns and the mysteries from ancient India to Greece. In *Isis Unveiled* she wrote: "Some writers deriving a curious analogy between the name of Orpheus and an old Greek term, ορφνός, dark or tawny-coloured, make him Hindu by connecting the term with his dusky Hindu complexion" (1877, 561n). She also suggested that Orpheus torn apart by the maenads symbolizes how truth is broken into pieces as it becomes popular and paradoxically more obscure.

White goddess historian Robert Graves thought the name a reference to the riverbank, like Bran the Blessed, King of the Island of the Mighty. Graves believed that the lyre Orpheus plucks was a later addition. He thought a flute, made from the reeds growing on the riverbank, was the actual instrument of Orpheus.

But as G. R. S. Mead wrote in the 1890s, "the name Orpheus is derived from the Egyptian, Hebrew, Phoenician, Assyrian, Arabic, Persian or Sanskrit, according to the taste or inventive faculty of the philological apologist." He added: "And no doubt there will be writers who will 'prove' that the name Orpheus is from radicals in Chinese, Eskimo, Maya, or even Volapük! There is very little that cannot be proved or disproved by such philology" (1965, 19). Volapük was a language a priest constructed after a dream in which God told him to create an international language. It didn't catch on.

Words with the same prefix in ancient Greek refer to the dark of murky night (*orphnaios*); a brown-gray color made from black mixed with a little white and red (*orphinus*); or orphan (*orphanos*). So the prefix *orph* tells us nothing we can be certain about.

Myth gives us two glimpses of him. The musician on the *Argo* whose music is stronger than the song of the Sirens. When Orpheus plays music, the fish jump from the ocean and birds hover in flocks. When the heroes, at sea too long, begin to bicker among themselves, Orpheus ends the trouble with a song about the creation of the world. As their oars churn the sea, his music urges them to epic efforts. Wherever the heroes on the *Argo* go, they establish cults, with Orpheus providing musical rites. Among his gifts to his followers was an unknown stone used to prevent seasickness.

But ancient Greeks also chuckled at the story that Orpheus wouldn't enter the contest for singers of hymns, competition in sacred matters being impure, according to him. Was he a coward, as Plato accuses? His sensitivity seemed a bit precious to people who worshipped gods who reveled in competition, like the tug of war in the *Iliad* between Zeus and all the other gods. Zeus won.

The other glimpse of Orpheus in myth is the more famous today, but was much less interesting to the ancient Greeks. Orpheus was to marry his love Eurydice, but on their wedding day she was attacked by a satyr. Fleeing his unwanted advances, she fell into a nest of vipers and died. Orpheus turned the world to tears as he sang his grief. The weeping gods advised him to go to the underworld to try for a miracle.

So Orpheus descended into the world of the dead. In Homer, the ghosts, like a swarm of shadows, are drawn to the blood sacrifice from which they draw enough strength to speak. But the song of Orpheus attracts huge crowds of ghosts. Not even the gods of the underworld could resist his song. The vulture stopped eating the liver of Prometheus. The vengeful Furies grew calm and reflective. Sisyphus stopped rolling his rock up the hill to listen. But what an awkward moment! The queen of the underworld, Persephone, is only there because her husband, Hades, abducted her. Her marriage began with rape. How could she deny Orpheus his wish? Eurydice fleeing an attacker would have reminded Persephone of herself.

The Romans liked to paint Hades as the skeptic in the situation, the only one unmoved by the song. But Persephone changed his mind. Hades, a shrewd judge of human character, had one last trick up his sleeve. Orpheus must not look back. He must have faith that Hades would be good to his word. But Orpheus couldn't bear it. He felt the presence of his lost Eurydice there just behind him. Fear overpowered him. Plato suggested Hades sent a ghost to impersonate Eurydice, to further shame this impudent mortal. Orpheus reached the sunlight, but instead of waiting with faith for his lover's touch, he turned to see she had not yet quite emerged from shadow.

On a mountaintop, heartbroken Orpheus sang songs to the sun at dawn. The Thracian men left their wives to study with him. In revenge, they say, the women tore Orpheus apart. Another story is told, that maenads ritually murdered Orpheus for tampering with the rites of Dionysus. They tore his head off. Trees suddenly lost all their leaves. The floating head, softly singing, passed weeping animals on a weeping river under a weeping sky. It floated to Lesbos, a large island in the Aegean Sea along the coast of Asia Minor. Lesbos, with high mountains and wide bays, exported wine, oil, and corn. Here Sappho reinvented lyric poetry and Terpander revolutionized music. At Lesbos, Apollo saved the head of Orpheus. Its tomb became a famous oracle of the dead. The nightingales that nested there were said to sing more sweetly.

So much for the Orpheus of pure myth. But the life of Orpheus only began with those vignettes. Then started the translation of the myth into philosophical literature and low-brow ritual for hire. Then began his long life in paintings and sculptures, in poems and fiction, his recurring inspiration to generation after generation of artists.

What did ancient writers have to say about Orpheus? Apollonius of Rhodes, author of the epic *Argonautica,* discussing Jason and the Argonauts, about Orpheus wrote ca. 300 BCE (the following translations are Ronnie's): "After devoting his youth to education he learned stories about the Gods. Then he went to Egypt, where he furthered his education and became the greatest man among the Greeks, for his knowledge of the Gods, and for his poems and songs. And because he so loved his wife he dared the amazing deed of descending into Hades where he enchanted Persephone with his song and convinced her to help him bring his wife back to Earth."

About two hundred years later, Diodorus, a historian from Sicily, at some time during the reigns of Julius Caesar and Emperor Augustus, wrote about Orpheus:

> I will say something about him. Dionysus gave gleaming-eyed Charops the kingdom of Thrace and the rites of Initiation. Oiagros inherited the kingdom, and the rites and passed them onto his son Orpheus. Orpheus, by training and natural gifts, was exceptional; he made many changes in the rites. For this reason the Initiations that were given by Dionysus came to be called Orphic. Orpheus is in culture, music and poetry easily the best of those we remember; he wrote astonishing, melodious poetry. They said he could move trees and animals with his song. He studied long. He learned to understand the myths of religion. Then he lived in Egypt where he learned so much more and so became the Greek expert on religion, ceremony, music and poetry. He was an Argonaut. For love of his wife he descended into Hades where he so charmed Persephone with his music she agreed to help him bring his wife back like another Dionysus, for they say Dionysus raised his mother Semele back to life from Hades.

As we shall soon see, however, there were skeptics among the ancients who left for our consideration their low opinions of all things Orphic.

Mysterious Orpheus

The careful reader can detect in the writing of ancient Egypt and ancient Greece a fear not only of offending the gods but of boring them. In the *Odyssey* the goddess Athena looks out for Odysseus because his cleverness delights her. She even takes the form of a swallow to fly frantically in the rafters while Odysseus kills the suitors who have dishonored his house.

For the Greeks the gods were near. The obscure ocean god Nereus was the grandfather of Achilles. In ancient Sicily slave soldiers carved the name of Zeus and a symbol of a thunderbolt on the stones they used in their slings. A man hit by lightning was "Zeus struck" and blessed with immortality in paradise, though all that was left of him was a smoldering body. Some scholars have argued that Zeus struck was the metaphor preferred by Orphics for purifying the soul, not unlike the *dorje* or thunderbolt of enlightenment of Tibetan Buddhism.

Artemis depicted on a vase painting about the defeat of the Persian emperor Darius had rich overtones of meaning for Athenians. They knew that the victory on land at Marathon that stopped the invasion from the east was fought on the day sacred to Artemis and that the small victory at sea near Artemision soon led to the decisive battle fought on water under a shining full moon. To the ancient Greeks these were clear signs that the goddess Artemis had helped them to defeat the Persians.

The early fifth century CE Roman antiquarian Macrobius wrote that the myth of the dismemberment of Dionysus was meant to illustrate how numbers reveal the way pure conscious being becomes divided up, whether into a universe or the parts of the human body. How can the signifier *Orphic* include both mathematical philosophy and the practices of Olympias, the mother of Alexander the Great? Olympias, Plutarch tells us, was "addicted to the Orphic rites," which she celebrated with her wild Thracian sisters, handling serpents—the ancient Greek version of the Pentecostals of Appalachia.

For the theosophists and Platonists of the late nineteenth and early twentieth century, the Orphic hymns were the actual lyrics of the musical performances of the Eleusinian mysteries. G. R. S. Mead's once authoritative book *Orpheus* followed Thomas Taylor's interpretation of second-century CE geographer Pausanias. Pausanias wrote of "Thracian Orpheus" that his hymns were not only few but succinct. The Lycomedes, an Athenian family dedicated to sacred music, knew them and sang them during the mysteries. Pausanius considers the Homeric hymns more elegant than the Orphic but he acknowledges that Greek religion revered the Orphic as more sacred.

This and other examples of provocative but misleading evidence were compiled by sincere scholars for generations to create the impression of a pagan church that once rivaled early Christianity. The theory was demolished by two classics of Orphic studies, W. K. C. Guthrie's *Orpheus and Greek Religion* (1935) and Ivan Linforth's *The Arts of Orpheus* (1941).

Guthrie examined the evidence and found that while the

hymns may have been used in some sort of organized ritual, this was not the liturgy of a once popular religion. He emphasized that even for the ancient writers, including Plato, the works of Orpheus were considered literature.

Guthrie also pointed out the significant differences between the Eleusinian and Orphic mysteries. Eleusis was a spectacle of light and color, theatrical apparitions and dramatic experiences that were intended to wake the soul and reinforce morality, an experience that was said to change initiates forever. The Orphics demanded disciplines of diet and other austerities and continual study. The initiates called themselves *mystai,* the origin of the English word *mystic.* The mysteries were an event that inspired some kind of transformative awakening. Orphism was a lifelong devotion. While the average person was aware of Orpheus and the mysteries, only a few really lived the Orphic life to achieve the full measure of self-knowledge. "Many carry the wand," a famous Orphic saying went, "but few are the Bakhoi," the mystically initiated, the spiritually awakened.

The earliest investigators found the hymns already hopelessly anonymous. Some ancient scholars argued that Pythagoras himself had written some of them, but the more common belief was that Pythagoras had learned his numerology from the Orphic mysteries. The Pythagorean prohibition against beans appears in the incense recipe for the *Hymn to Gaia,* to Earth. But that hardly qualifies as evidence. How do we differentiate between what might be called literary influence, or poetic appropriation of a metaphor, and genuine identity of content and practice?

The Nobel Prize–winning mathematician and philosopher Bertrand Russell had some things to say on this subject:

The Orphics were an ascetic sect; wine, to them, was only a symbol, as, later, in the Christian sacrament. The intoxication that they sought was that of "enthusiasm," of union with the god. They believed themselves, in this way, to acquire mystic knowledge not obtainable by ordinary means. This mystical element entered into Greek philosophy with Pythagoras, who was a reformer of Orphism as Orpheus was a reformer of the religion of Dionysus. From Pythagoras Orphic elements entered into the philosophy of Plato, and from Plato into most later philosophy that was in any degree religious. (Russell 1946, 37)

But his confidence in his facts proved to be premature as further research blurred the distinctions he tried to set so clearly.

Then we must consider the question of where Pythagoras got his wisdom. Was he simply a superior soul with a divine intellect as many would later argue? Pythagoras was said to have studied with the priests of the temples of ancient Egypt. The similarities between the community he established and the traditions of the Egyptian temples include vows of secrecy, rites of purification, and the ban on eating beans. The Neoplatonist Porphyry claimed that in Egypt Pythagoras perfected the geometry he had learned from Thales and Anaximander. Yet the Greek sages Epimenides and Pherecydes taught reincarnation before there were Pythagoreans and Orphics. Both were said to have been teachers of Pythagoras.

But then we must deal with the question of why Pythagoras wore pants. In those days only the Iranians in Persia wore pants. They had also inherited the great mathematical knowledge of the Babylonian Empire. Persia and Samos, the home of Pythagoras, had a long history of diplomatic relations, trade deals, and sharing technology, arts, and crafts. Some of the famous discoveries of Pythagoras had already been discovered by the astrologers of Babylon. Persia could be another possible source of the ideas we call Pythagorean.

The usually reliable sixth-century CE scholar Philoponus wrote that Aristotle credited a poet named Onomacritus with inventing or reforming the Orphic writings, including the hymns and the *Orphic Theogony,* in his *Holy Words of Orpheus,* in Athens around 500 BCE, making Onomacritus a younger contemporary of Pythagoras.

Joannes Tzetzes (ca. 1150 CE), the Greek grammarian of Constantinople, claimed Onomacritus was one of those who arranged the books of Homer under Peisistratos, but we don't know what convinced him of that.

Peisistratos was a benevolent tyrant of Athens who protected small farmers. His ambitious building program included a majestic temple of Olympian Zeus. During his reign, Attic coins and black-figure pottery (a style of painting on Greek vases, ca. seventh through fifth century BCE, that featured dark figures and ornaments in silhouette against a red background) achieved prominence throughout the Greek world. After the death of Peisistratos, his eldest son, Hippias, ruled Athens. Poetry, sculpture, and architecture flourished under the patronage of Hipparchus, the younger brother of Hippias. Hipparchus encouraged the development of red-figure pottery, which flourished from the late sixth to late fourth century BCE and was the reverse of black-figure pottery, with red figures and ornaments against a black background. The *Oxford Classical Dictionary* summed him up neatly as "frivolous and amorous."

Herodotus records that Hipparchus was a friend and patron to Onomacritus. Lasus of Hermione, a rival poet under the wing of the Athenian tyrants, accused Onomacritus of adding his own verses to the sacred oracles of Musaeus. Musaeus was said to have been a great oracular poet, a historian, a maker of holy rites, a philosopher, a musician, and a high priest of the mysteries of Demeter during the time of Hercules.

In his *Protagoras,* Plato calls Musaeus a prophet. Socrates in the

Apology says: "What would we give if we could talk with Orpheus and Musaeus, Hesiod and Homer? No, if it's true, I would gladly die repeatedly." Was this a witty reference by Socrates to the allegedly Orphic belief in reincarnation? Aristotle quotes Musaeus in book 8 of his *Politics:* "To mortals of all the things the sweetest is song."

A few hundred years later, Diodorus of Sicily claimed that Musaeus was the son of Orpheus. Perhaps "son of Orpheus" was an honorable designation for someone especially inspired. For some reason the early church father Clement of Alexandria wrote that Musaeus taught Orpheus, instead of the other way around. Or, perhaps he was sleepy the night he wrote that.

Tampering with the oracles was an act of sacrilege, so Hipparchus banished Onomacritus. Here history loses track of him for a time. Hipparchus was eventually assassinated. The *Oxford Classical Dictionary* hints: "Personal vices led to his murder." Hippias tightened his grip, but beset by Persians to the north cutting off his gold supply in Thrace and Spartans attacking from the south, he fled Athens. He reappeared at the court of Xerxes, with none other than Onomacritus, whom he had brought with him to read omens for the great king of the First Persian Empire.

By command of Hippias, Onomacritus was careful to read only the omens favorable for an invasion of Greece. Xerxes promised to restore Hippias to the throne. Old Hippias stood with Xerxes when the Spartan king Leonidas, three hundred of his guard, and five thousand Spartan Helots, Arcadians, Corinthians, Thespians, and Thebans held back perhaps three hundred thousand Persians for three days at Thermopylae. Some historians say Hippias was killed when the Athenian fleet defeated Xerxes in the narrow straits. We know nothing of the fate of Onomacritus.

In a note to his third lecture, "Mythical Preliminary Stage of Philosophy," Nietzsche wrote: "Orpheus was the manifestation of the Dionysus ruling Hades: Zagreus. The name suggests darkness, and thus descent into the underworld: Orpheus is torn apart by Maenads; Zagreus, by Titans. The hymns of the ancient Orphic mysteries were inspirational. The accepted belief that the Orphic mysteries began after Homer is most questionable. Homer's silence may be because the spirit of Homeric poetry contradicts the Orphic. As the sixth century began, Orphic doctrines were rewritten, by Onomacritus and Orpheus of Croton, to conform with folk beliefs." Croton was the city in which Pythagoras established his school, leading some to wonder if Orpheus of Croton was a pseudonym for Pythagoras. Lebedev (2002) suggests that Suda's quote from Asclepiades of Myrlea claiming Orpheus of Croton lived in Athens at the court of Peisistratos could make Orpheus of Croton a pseudonym for Onomacritus himself.

Pausanias believed Onomacritus invented the myth of the Titans who covered their faces with quicklime before murdering Dionysus (the word *titanos* meant "quicklime"). Zeus punished their abduction, murder, and cannibalism of the infant Dionysus with lightning bolts. From the electrified fusion of the flesh of Dionysus and of the Titans, human beings were born. Every human is a confusion of Dionysus and Titan. The Dionysus part is immortal, beautiful, serene, wise, and of the race of the stars. The Titan part is mortal, anguished, rebellious, violent, and deceitful.

How then can we restore the divine Dionysian part of ourselves? According to Damascius, the last of the Neoplatonists and the last director of the Platonic school in Athens, that is the job of Apollo. Damascius was born in Syria; he was one of the pagan philosophers persecuted by the Christian emperor Justinian I. In his commentary on Plato's *Phaedo*, Damascius wrote: "When Dionysus had projected his reflection into the mirror, he followed it, and was thus scattered over the universe. Apollo gathers him and brings him back to heaven, for he is the purifying god and truly the savior of Dionysus, and therefore he is celebrated as the 'Dionysus-Giver'" (Edmonds 2009, 518, n23).

In two words: *soma sema*. A play on words in Greek that associates the body (*soma*) with a tomb (*sema*), the body as tomb. The Greek word *lethe* means "forgetfulness" or "oblivion" and is related to the English word *lethargy*. Forgetfulness is the Orphic evil. Knowledge is memory and liberation. The Greek for truth, *alethia,* means "without oblivion" or "without forgetfulness."

We live many lives purging the Titan, learning not to give in to lust for power, cruelty, envy, and deceit. From this point of view, the Orphics taught catharsis through a course of abstinence, purification, and self-discipline, not unlike Jain yoga and the practices of the medieval Cathar sect that led to the Albigensian crusade. The sacred drunken frenzy of the wild followers of Dionysus could now be replaced by rites of purification, spiritual enthusiasm, and ecstasy, the Orphic *enthousiasmos* (to have a God within) and *ekstasis* (to stand outside oneself in trance).

However, as we shall see, modern scholars have questioned whether this belief, and the story of the Titanic origin of the human race, are truly Orphic. Those we call Orphics did not refer to themselves as such. Ivan M. Linforth, professor of Greek at the University of California, Berkeley, published his influential *The Arts of Orpheus* in 1941. That year the Nazi war machine appeared invincible as it roared across Russia on its way to the certain doom of Russian winter. Japanese plans for the surprise attack on Pearl Harbor were about to succeed.

Linforth deconstructed the connection between Orphic artifacts as they are and the myth of the murder of Dionysus, reminding us that we know very little about the literary and artistic remains associated with Orphic cult. We have no proof that the myth of Dionysus and the Titans was Orphic, Linforth argued, if indeed the Orphic cult was anything more than a convenient signifier for miscellaneous beliefs and practices considered outside the Olympian religious establishment.

Sympathetic scholars of earlier eras held up the Titanic origin of humanity as a foreshadowing of the Christian belief in original sin. To make matters more complicated, the idea that Orpheus taught reincarnation originated from the slightest evidence. Olympiodorus, whom we shall meet again, was the last leader of the Neoplatonists and is our only source when identifying the Titan story as Orphic. An Italian scholar by the name of Domenico Comparetti on the basis of writings by Olympiodorus tied together Orphic fragments, including the rare golden leaves. From this "evidence" Comparetti stated that Orpheus taught reincarnation. Maybe he did. The problem is exemplified by a bone funerary tablet that bears the message:

Life Death Life
Truth

If we believe that rebirth understood as reincarnation is an Orphic doctrine, rather than simply a motto of Dionysus the savior, there could be no clearer statement. Between each life we live there is a death. But the inscription could also mean that after this life ends, we have an afterlife, a return to where we came from. There we encounter the truth about life and ourselves.

Another educated guess at the time and place of origin of the songs of Orpheus as we have them is near Pergamon in western Asia Minor, on the west coast of what we now call Turkey, not far from where the great Sufi poet Rumi grew up. Asiatic deities addressed in the hymns, Melinoe, Hipta, Mise, are foreign to the

19

ancient Greeks and were found only in the hymns, until an archaeological dig in 1910 discovered inscriptions mentioning them.

No one is sure if there ever was an Orpheus or Orphic mysteries. It could all have been a literary hoax embroidered upon over
many centuries. But let us return to the question at hand. If not
Onomacritus, then who was the author of the Orphic hymns?
Perhaps imagine an aristocratic or priestly antiquarian working
with various texts, some ancient, some more recent, compiling the
formulas and sayings, possibly to please a powerful woman in the
imperial court. What sort of world did this antiquarian live in?

The notorious Pax Romana, two centuries of relative peace
and prosperity under the aqueducts, the laws, and the boots of the
Roman Empire, had recently come to an end. At the height of the
power of Rome, the Pax Romana produced as close as Rome would
get to Plato's philosopher-king, Marcus Aurelius, whose *Meditations*
are still read today by people seeking to live better lives.

But then the bubonic plague struck. The Antonine plague
was the worst pandemic to reach Rome in a hundred years.
Brought back by legions returning from the Near East, the plague
killed one out of four who became sick, in the cities and among
the legions. Across the empire, twenty-five million people died.
Marcus held the imperial administration together, but the dam-
age had been done. Then his son and successor, the emperor
Commodus, revealed himself to be more insane than Caligula.

Instead of governing during a crisis, Commodus named a
month of the year after himself. He claimed to have defeated ten
thousand fighters, left-handed, presumably not all at once. He had
himself depicted in coins and statues as Hercules. Meanwhile, he
sold public offices to the highest bidder. Unlike the film *Gladiator,*
Commodus was strangled in his bath by a professional wrestler.

At a distant military camp, the news must have brought a

sense of relief to a half-Italian, half-African senator and army general named Septimus Severus. Commodus had noticed the popularity Severus enjoyed with his legions. But the new emperor was a friend and ally of Severus.

The good times didn't last long. The Praetorian Guard considered the new emperor too cheap and too severe, a recurring theme we will find. After his assassination, the wealthiest man in Rome simply bought the imperial throne from the Praetorian Guard.

When the legions who defended the Danube River heard about the throne being sold to the highest bidder, they expressed their outrage by declaring Severus emperor and marching to Rome. What followed was the Year of Five Emperors, a bloody civil war that further weakened the Roman Empire. Severus emerged victorious, and the short-lived dynasty he established may well have been the birthplace of the Orphic hymns as we have them.

The Severan Dynasty

The first thing Septimus Severus did when he became emperor was to remove all the old Praetorian Guard, replacing them with loyal veterans from his Danube legions. Most scholars agree, Severus so embroiled the military in imperial politics that he established the conditions that would lead to the fall of the empire.

Throughout his reign, Severus spurned the demands of the citizens and the senate, who despised him as a dark-skinned "barbarian," pointing out ruefully that a countryman of their hated enemy Hannibal now sat on the imperial throne.

For ten years Severus tolerated all religions, but then he ordered severe penalties on the practice of Christianity, and he closed the key Christian school at Alexandria. Some have argued that he feared the popularity of a religion that preached peace while he was busy burdening the empire with ever increasing war debt.

For the story of the Orphic hymns, Severus may be less important than his wife Julia Domna, the first of the famous four Julias of Rome: extraordinary Syrian women who for nearly twenty-two years guided the empire during the greatest challenges, while avoiding the threats that would inevitably engulf Rome after the last Julia was killed.

The first Julia was Julia Domna, or Black Julia, since *domna* means "black." She had grown up in the Holy Precincts of the Phoenician sun god Elagabal, but we will use the more traditional and picturesque name: the Temple of Baal. Her father was a high priest living in splendor that would have made Louis XIV, the Sun King, blush. Her ancestors had been not just high priests but kings, until Rome forbade her family from ruling both politics and religion.

Domna married Severus when she was seventeen and he was forty-two. Ancient historians wondered if Severus married her because her horoscope, according to skilled Babylonian astrologers, indicated she would marry a man who would rule the world.

As Severus climbed the rungs of power, Julia Domna left her life of extreme luxury to live with her husband, first in the governor's more humble palace in Gaul and then in military camps and border forts, from the deserts of Parthia to the highlands of Scotland. He respected her advice, impressed by her education and intelligence. Their first son, the future emperor Caracalla, was born in a military camp.

Domna must have been elated when she moved with her husband into the imperial palace of Rome. But all too quickly eleven years of happy marriage ended. Severus had a childhood friend named Plautianus whom he trusted enough to appoint not only commander of the Praetorian Guard, but also chief administrator supervising the tedious work of running the empire. The first emperor Augustus had famously said that he was no more than a glorified accountant.

But Plautianus did not deserve his old friend's trust. He gaslit Severus with rumors about Domna's infidelities. Perhaps insecure due to the age difference between himself and Julia Domna, Severus believed his scheming friend, not his faithful wife.

To avoid a dangerous scandal, the couple pretended that all was well while privately they were no longer civil. Domna was given honors beyond other Roman empresses, but her advice was no longer welcome. She was convinced that Plautianus would one day seize power and kill them all.

When Augustus ascended his throne, he assembled the greatest talents from around the empire, hosting a salon that included the most famous of all Roman poets, Virgil, whom we will meet again. Virgil would visit Augustus and his wife, the notorious Empress Livia, to read his latest poems to them.

Domna and the three other Julias, her sister Maesa, her niece Soaemias, and her grandniece Mammaea, presided over a sophisticated cosmopolitan culture. The salons Domna hosted were attended by luminaries whose books deeply influenced the evolution of European culture. Guests at her salon included Apuleius, the author of the groundbreaking satirical novel *The Golden Ass;* Galen, whose medical works were considered indispensable for more than a thousand years; Cassius Dio, the senator and chronicler of the times, who wrote "our age of Silver now turned to Iron and Rust"; and Philostratus, whom Domna commissioned to write his delightful but fanciful life of the pagan sage Apollonius of Tyana.

A letter from Philostratus to Domna survives. It begins: "To the Empress Julia. Divine Plato never envied the sophists, though some say confidently that he did. He imitated them, since they went on journeys in charming cities, both big and small, like an Orpheus" (Penella 1979). Other surviving letters by Philostratus reflect the fascination with Egypt and India that alarmed Roman traditionalists already outraged by Severus and Domna's openness to foreign influences. Domna's heritage seemed to threaten Rome with a priest-king, such as a pharaoh or the high priest-kings of Baal. Many Romans feared that the grandson of a high priest of

Baal might demand to hold both titles on the imperial throne, and in fact, as we shall see, Domna's grandnephew did.

After seven years of pretending their marriage was happy, the imperial couple, who had once sincerely loved one another, were reunited. Severus had a brother who was involved in the plot against Domna. On his deathbed he confessed. Then Domna and Caracalla accused Plautianus of plotting to assassinate them and Severus. The trial of the emperor's old friend ended abruptly with his execution—a tricky situation as Plautianus's daughter was Caracalla's wife. Caracalla took the opportunity to banish her and was rumored to have had her killed.

Severus appointed a new commander of the Praetorian Guard, a genius in the area of jurisprudence whose reforms would establish what we today call classical Roman law, the foundation for the legal systems of Europe and its colonies to this day.

Many senators seemed to have been involved in the plot against the Severans. Severus became a threat to them. They were watched carefully. Enough executions occurred, and often enough, that the composition of the senate changed.

The happiness that Domna must have felt at her vindication and the renewal of her husband's trust was no doubt disturbed by her concern over the hostility her two sons felt toward each other. Caracalla and his younger brother, Geta, dared suggest that when their father died the empire be split in half to avoid a civil war. Domna warned them that the empire must be held together at all costs.

With Rome properly subdued, Domna traveled with her husband and sons over the English Channel to the island province of Britannia. Severus led his armies deeper into what became England than any Roman army had reached before, all the way into Caledonia, which we call northern Scotland today. He forced the Picts and their Druids to ask for peace. They would be left alone in the highlands, Severus offered, but the lowlands would be made productive by herdsmen and farmers, who must live without fear of attack. The Picts had no choice but to agree to the terms of this half-African Roman emperor and his wife, the daughter of a high priest of Baal. They were certainly unlike the emperors their ancestors had faced: Julius Caesar and Claudius. We can easily imagine the empress questioning the Druids about their beliefs and practices.

But the deal that would have completed the conquest of Britannia was negotiated from a litter. The emperor was not well. He died in that forlorn military camp, surrounded by his sons and adoring wife. His final words were to Caracalla and Geta: "Get along with each other. Enrich the soldiers. Scorn the rest."

With the death of the emperor, the Picts, and other tribes with them, considered all agreements void. Caracalla spent a year fighting to force the Britons to keep the deals they made with his father, but then he returned to Rome, to take sole possession of the throne he had shared with Severus and Geta.

Domna's pleas and warnings to her sons fell on deaf ears. In fact, the meeting that she brokered between them led to tragedy. Sources differ. Some say Caracalla stabbed his brother himself. Others that the Praetorian Guard did the dirty work. Drenched in her younger son's blood, Domna held Geta as he died in her lap.

The heartbroken mother was not allowed to mourn her son. Her friend Cassius Dio wrote: "They compelled her to rejoice, laughing as if good fortune had occurred. Her words, gestures, and the changes of color of her skin were closely observed." Twenty thousand of Geta's associates, his inner circle and all closely connected to them, were executed by the new emperor.

Caracalla convinced the senate to issue a *damnatio memoriae* (condemnation of memory) against his brother. All images of Geta and his name were removed from coins, monuments, and all other public records. Having accomplished that, Caracalla left Rome. He would never return.

Caracalla was a soldier like his father, but unlike his father, he was a notorious tyrant. He is depicted with a threatening scowl in his portraits from coins to statues. Like most tyrants he did not take ridicule kindly.

His personality can perhaps best be illustrated by his reaction to a popular satirical comedy produced in Alexandria that mocked him, especially the idea that he had killed his brother in self-defense, as he claimed. Several years later when Caracalla traveled to the east he stopped at Alexandria. The leading citizens who greeted him at the gate were promptly slaughtered. Then Caracalla unleashed his legions to rape, loot, and plunder the city, a process that required several days.

In need of more money for wars and influenced by his mother, Caracalla's *Constitutio Antoniniana* gave citizenship to all free men across the empire. Romans were not happy with the sudden confusion over what it meant to be a citizen and a Roman. A distinct and proud racial tradition had become a universal ideal. Foreigners had competed for power by merit in Rome, and they had now attained the throne and declared themselves Romans.

Because her son was only interested in war, Domna took his place, lending her good advice to the committees that ran the administration of the empire. Some have argued that it was she in her role as substitute imperial judge who established the highest standards of Roman law. The people loved and respected her. She had not only proven her intelligence, she seemed to have their interests and the fate of the empire at heart. But Caracalla's rule ended abruptly.

Six years after he murdered his brother to prevent yet another Roman civil war, Caracalla was assassinated by an ambitious soldier who became disgruntled when he was not made a centurion. He was put up to it by a praetorian commander named Macrinus. Macrinus knew that Caracalla had grown suspicious of the power he himself had given him in the city of Rome. He struck before Caracalla could. Declared the new emperor, Macrinus sent Domna and her sister Maesa back home to Syria, where they were under unusually luxurious house arrest.

The sadness and bitterness of Domna became proverbial. She and Severus had believed in the Roman dream of a world of common laws and trade, where all beliefs and heritages would be respected. She did not believe that Macrinus could hold the throne. The civil war she and Severus had prevented would now become inevitable. She knew she was too dangerous to be allowed to live and expected the command for her execution at any moment. Stricken with a slow, painful, and fatal disease, she starved herself to death, dying only months after her son Caracalla.

The reign of Macrinus lasted only a year. He tried to be a good emperor. You'd think the senate would be delighted to have a Roman aristocrat on the throne again, but no, he was merely a knight, so they doubted him. Macrinus imposed unpopular new rules meant to save money. Despite the good sense of his administration, the Praetorian Guard and the Roman legions weren't happy about pay cuts. They were accustomed to the more than generous military budgets of Severus and Caracalla. Not only that, but Macrinus paid an enormous ransom to end the long Parthian war. Even the citizens of Rome were outraged. Some of them could still remember the glorious triumph of Severus displaying the wealth he had plundered from the capital of Parthia. However, unfortunately for Rome, that victory ironically led to the revival of its greatest enemy, the Persian Empire.

Maesa saw her opportunity. A wealthy widow now, she recruited her grandson Elagabalus, a fourteen-year-old boy who had inherited the office of high priest of Baal.

Not only is Elagabalus a difficult name to pronounce, it isn't even his real name. The names we have for him are ceremonial. Elagabalus was one of the names of the god he served. When pronouncing it, we can combine the eleg- of elegant with the -abulous of fabulous.

With the help of local senators and other prominent allies, Maesa bribed the nearby Third Legion, known as the Gallic, for having served Julius Caesar in his wars in Gaul. Their mascot was a bull, the symbol of Caesar, their founder. Rumors were spread that Elagabalus was actually the illegitimate son of Caracalla. Maesa had the boy's hair cut and his clothes tailored à la Caracalla. Since there was a natural resemblance between the second cousins, the plan could work.

Maesa's allies tried to convince the legions that their oath to obey Caracalla now applied to Elagabalus, therefore making Macrinus a usurper of the Severan dynasty. Maesa, Elagabalus, and their inner circle were brought to the camp of the Third Legion where they were hailed. To his delight, the new emperor was provided with robes of imperial purple. This Trojan horse of a candidate for emperor could not have been more different from Caracalla.

Macrinus convinced the senate to declare war on the adolescent barbarian upstart. Then he traveled to Syria. He may have thought this rebellion in the city of the Temple of Baal a minor challenge. He sent not a legion but a troop of cavalry led by a respected general, confident that order would be restored. When considering the outcome of the battle that followed, we are left to wonder if word got out that Elagabalus paid soldiers well. The vast wealth of the temple belonged to him by inheritance. The soldiers were still grumbling about how cheap Macrinus was. The cavalry killed its officers and joined Elagabalus, who no doubt rewarded them handsomely.

In Syria, Macrinus visited the Second Legion, known as Parthica, formed by Emperor Severus himself for service in the Roman-Parthian Wars. Their mascot was a centaur. He promised a five-figure bonus, four figures to be paid up front.

At the border of Syria the legions clashed. But history repeated itself. Despite the recent generosity of Macrinus, the legion Parthica proved loyal to the house of Severus. Only the Praetorian Guard remained with Macrinus as he escaped to Antioch. But Elagabalus was right behind him.

Outside Antioch, Macrinus had no choice but to face the superior force of Elagabalus. Macrinus had a clever strategy. The guards would remove their heavy armor and use a lighter shield. Their increased maneuverability would give them an advantage. Macrinus must have felt confident as he watched the Praetorian Guard fight their way deep into the lines of the rebel legions. The legions wavered as many soldiers turned to flee. In a chariot Maesa stood with her daughter Soaemias. Soaemias knew that her son's life was in the balance.

Soaemias jumped from the chariot. She ran toward the battle rallying the troops. Maesa, the sister of Domna could do no less. Mother and daughter ran toward certain death at the hands of the Praetorian Guard. Perhaps there were veterans among the legion founded by Serverus that remembered him. Macrinus watched the legions loyal to Elagabalus turn to fight. Apparently, he didn't think the Praetorian Guard had much of a chance, since he fled. Seeing that, the guard stopped fighting and swore loyalty to the new new emperor.

Two other legions thought they had their own candidates for emperor, but those rebellions were crushed with an aggression that Macrinus had perhaps not wished to use against fellow Romans. Trouble began when Elagabalus sent papers to the senate declaring himself emperor. The senate was supposed to initiate that process. But then there was that painting the emperor sent. An absurd and garish portrait of a fourteen-year-old boy wearing the heavy facial makeup and fabulous robes of the high priest of Baal. The new emperor ordered the portrait hung on the wall in the senate to represent him until his arrival.

Perhaps of all the offenses committed by their new emperor, the senators resented most his violation of the traditional exclusion of women from the senate. Elagabalus gave his mother and grandmother the right to not just attend but to address the senators as the emperor's representatives.

As for the emperor he was busy with "frenzied orgies," which he called religious rites. Rumor had it that animals were involved in the highly questionable rituals. The most reprehensible behavior was being excused as sacred practice. But is this accurate history? It sounds like the usual Roman propaganda about barbarians from the east.

Some interesting details about Elagabalus may be true, though they are so strange we may doubt it. For example, he is credited with the invention of what has come to be called a whoopee cushion. And the cushion was used correctly, placed upon the chairs of only the most pompous guests. Elagabalus was a practical joker. But his jokes could be cruel, with tragic consequences, if the story is true that he had so many flowers dropped on his dinner guests some suffocated.

Elagabalus would seem to be the world's first Surrealist. He demanded snow in his summer garden. He had a dinner for bald men only. Another for men with only one eye. And a dinner for very overweight men with couches too small for them, causing much hilarity as they tried to stay seated during the sumptuous feast. Elagabalus hosted dinners where all the food was red. Another of green foods only, or white.

Maesa and Soaemias could inspire rebellions and rally legions to victory, but they could not convince the new emperor to act like a Roman. When encouraged to marry and to father an heir as soon as possible, Elagabalus married and divorced every year of his four-year reign. His second wife was a vestal virgin. "I am your sun god," he declared, "and she is your goddess of the moon." Most alarming to Rome, he demoted the Roman father god Jupiter and replaced him in the great temple with Baal, whom he married to all the goddesses of the Roman pantheon. Many sacred objects of Baal, including the great black stone, were moved into the Temple of Jupiter.

While Maesa provided the imperial oversight needed to make the empire function, Elagabalus was said to have offered offices, despicable acts of crime, and even himself to the highest bidder. He was not the first emperor to dress as a woman and pretend to have a husband, nor was he the first to prostitute himself in bars and brothels, but he may have been the first transgender person in recorded history. Not only did he prefer to dress as a woman, demanding the use of the pronoun *she,* she also offered a fortune to any doctor who could change her gender. She was said to have a husband, a former slave and chariot driver. We are told she liked to be called his wife. However, we are again left to wonder how much of this is reliable history and how much Roman propaganda against an emperor too eccentric for their tastes. Some of it appears to have been misunderstanding. The frenzied orgies may have been the wild dancing of the cult. The scandal of an emperor with an "effeminate" parasol was not scandalous in the East, where rulers often carried them for shade.

Four years into her grandson's reign, Maesa seems to have realized that neither the senate nor the Praetorian Guard were going to tolerate Elagabalus much longer. But Maesa had another grandson. Alexander Severus, thirteen years old, had been raised to conduct himself like a Roman by Maesa's other daughter Mammaea. Maesa began to pressure Elagabalus to adopt Alexander as successor. If Elagabalus wouldn't father an heir, then one must be appointed, for the security of his throne and of Rome. Elagabalus tried to have Alexander assassinated.

Soaemias, who had been content to let her mother run things in the palace, in Rome, and in the empire, seems to have come to her senses. She prevailed upon the emperor to wear a toga instead of a gorgeous robe. The Preatorian Guard were fine with Maesa running the empire. She was doing a good job of standing in for her grandson. But they cast their eyes now on Alexander. He couldn't be worse than Elagabalus. Rumors began spreading that Alexander was another bastard son of Caracalla.

When the emperor was about to make another attempt on the life of Alexander, the Praetorian Guard struck first. They found Elagabalus hiding from them by a toilet. Soaemias shielded her child's body with her own. They were both stabbed repeatedly. A story was told that the Praetorians tried to push the dead emperor's body through the toilet into the sewer, but they couldn't manage it. Both corpses were stripped naked, dragged through the streets of Rome, and dumped in the river. Historians have wondered whether Maesa was responsible for the assassination of the grandson she had put on the throne. The senators insisted that Maesa and Mammaea stay away from the senate. A special committee would convey their advice to the senators.

Julia Mammaea now took center stage. In Rome her sister Soaemias had been thought untrustworthy, but Mammaea was a dutiful woman. Of course, the army viewed the new emperor with suspicion, considering his predecessor. Nevertheless, his reign lasted thirteen years. The soldiers learned to respect him in small ways. He was an honest emperor, modest and honorable. He had simple habits. But everyone knew Maesa was the one truly in charge of the empire.

With the guidance of Maesa, Alexander restored Jupiter's great temple, returning the sacred objects of Baal to Syria. The other policies of Elagabalus were quickly removed. Romans were reassured.

The men Alexander and Maesa put into power, especially the legal expert Ulpian, whom they made commander of the Praetorian Guard, revolutionized Roman jurisprudence again. A soldier could now free slaves and name heirs in a will. His property would remain his no matter how long he was away at war. Greedy relatives were prevented from taking over ownership.

The reign of Alexander was a time of projects to improve Rome. Government buildings and the processes inside them were modernized. The baths were restored and became known as the Baths of Alexander. But then Maesa died. Mammaea was not like her mother and grandmother. She lacked their vision and decisiveness. Her son had been raised among the women, not in military camps.

Like the Julias, Alexander showed interest in all religions. The story that he wanted to build a temple for Jesus Christ is probably propaganda, but he did encourage the construction of a synagogue in Rome. He presented the congregation with a rare Torah from the collection of treasures of conquest. He believed all religions represented one truth.

Unfortunately, Ulpian was too much of a throwback to old Roman discipline for the Praetorian Guard. One night they got drunk and chased him down into the very chamber where the young emperor stood with his mother. They murdered Ulpian in front of Alexander and Mammaea. The last of the Severan emperors was viewed with suspicion, and all around him candidates for emperor plotted.

The story of their deaths was told in different ways. In one Alexander was simply killed at a meeting of his generals. The following romantic tale perhaps smacks too much of Roman propaganda. Mammaea heard in her tent the drunken angry soldiers. She convinced Alexander to go out and address them. He would remind them of Severus and Caracalla. He would remind them how they had rights now they never had before.

The drunken troops heckled him. "Miser! Weakling!" They chased him away. When sufficiently drunk, they marched to the emperor's tent where they found him and his mother holding on to each other. They hacked them to pieces. This story would seem to be a throwback to the murder of Dionysus by the Titans and of Orpheus by the maenads.

The Roman Empire had been governed by four Syrian princesses of the family that ruled the Temple of Baal, from the time when Caracalla had begun losing interest in anything but war in about 213 until the death of Alexander Severus in 234.

Mystical cults flourished during the Severan dynasty, above all the cult of Dionysus. Some modern scholars argue that the Orphic hymns may have been used at banquets, frequented by the Julias and their inner circle, where feasting and drinking, discussing philosophy even then considered ancient, along with an erotic appreciation of life, were given a spiritual purpose, by the intent of the hymns, to ask for grace from the divine.

Are the hymns ordered to facilitate a successful all-nighter? Some scholars think so. The heaviest drinking, they suspect, and the greatest risk of erotic distractions occurred during the series of hymns about two-thirds of the way through the cycle. The proceedings are brought to a close with sobering topics, such as the hymn to death. In this cosmopolitan atmosphere, the editor of the hymns as we have them may not have practiced the purifications and abstinence of the actual rites. These connoisseurs were sampling the delicacies of the mysteries.

If the Severan dynasty inspired an Orphic revival, and Vinogradov was right when he argued that the Athenian tyrants used the Orphic works of Onomacritus to support their regime, we may wonder if Orphism served the elite, never the people. But Lebedev (2022) argues persuasively that the evidence points rather to Orphics as wandering fortune tellers with as little political power as the beggars they were compared with. He agrees with Bremmer that Orphism was the literary invention of the Pythagoreans. A way to bring their wisdom to the common folk, while their mathematical mysticism was reserved for initiates.

Historians call what happened after the Severan dynasty the Crisis of the Third Century. Fifty years of civil war, breakdown of institutions, plagues and starvation caused by changes of climate. Some emperors reigned for only months or weeks. The hymns of Orpheus disappeared once again into obscurity.

The Pagan Orpheus

The Roman poets Virgil (ca. 50 BCE) and Ovid (ca. 1 CE) recast the myth of Orpheus with an emphasis on the tragic love story and especially the backward glance. But Ovid blamed Orpheus for introducing homosexuality to Greece because of a song he sang about a red-lipped boy on the ship Argo. Also during the reign of Augustus, a myth collector named Conon from Cappadocia, a Greek province in what is now Turkey, wrote:

> In the old days prophets played music. Orpheus, the son of Oiagros, and of the Muse Calliope, was king of the Macedonians and Odyrsai. He was skilled in music, especially the lyre. Since Thracians and Macedonians love music, they favored him. He was torn to pieces by the women of Thrace and Macedonia because he would not let them join his rites.
>
> Or it may have been for another reason, for they say Orpheus hated women after the death of his wife. On certain days a crowd of armed Thracians and Macedonians would gather in a big temple at Leibethra, the city on the Macedonian side of Mount Olympus. They would lay their

weapons down before entering. The angry women took the swords. They killed anyone who tried to overpower them. They tore Orpheus to pieces and threw the pieces into the sea. They did not repent, so plague struck.

An oracle told them to find the head of Orpheus and respectfully bury it. A fisherman finally showed it to them at the mouth of the river Meles. It was singing and had suffered no violence or decay; it was fresh and had the bloom of blood in it. They buried it under a great mound and fenced off the place. First a hero shrine, it grew into a temple. No woman may set foot in it.*

Orpheus became a popular decorating theme in ancient Rome. The musical emperor Nero owned glossy red trays depicting him. The face of Orpheus decorated jewelry, mirrors, plates, villa walls, villa floors, in paint and mosaic, his gaze always turned upward to the sky.

Theophrastus is never so well remembered as his teachers Plato and Aristotle, but his book the *Characters* deserves to be. Its gritty portraits of the various moralities of humans has much in common with the likes of Allen Ginsberg and Celine. He would seem to indicate a more organized Orphic religious experience. He paints an unflattering picture of the followers of Orpheus:

The Superstitious Man washes his hands in three springs, sprinkles himself with water from a temple fountain, puts a laurel leaf in his mouth, and then is ready for his day. If a weasel runs across his path he will not continue until someone else walks the ground or he has thrown three stones across the road. If a rat nibbles through a bag of barley, he

---

*Translation by Ronnie Pontiac.

goes to the expert on sacred law and asks what he must do. If the answer is he should get it sewn up he ignores the advice and performs a sacrifice to avoid harm. He purifies his house frequently, claiming it is haunted by Hekate, Goddess of ghosts and witches. He would never step on a tombstone or go anywhere near a dead body, or a woman in childbirth, for fear of contamination. If he has a dream he visits not only dream interpreters but also seers and those who read the omens of birds, to ask which god or goddess to pray to. Every month he attends the ritual of the Orphic sacrament, accompanied by his children, and his wife, or if she is occupied elsewhere, the nurse.*

Just as Kerouac and Whitman claimed holy revelation for their torrents of writing, recasting the known world from a new perspective, reversing long-established models, and bringing light to previously dark corners, so too could the Orphics walk among men with the burning eyes of visionaries who see beyond the preoccupations of mundane ambitions and desires: lucid dreamers, smiling at the phantoms so busy with their phantasms, the very essence of counterculture attitude.

In ancient Greece all citizens could claim at least a distant relation to the founding heroes of their cultures, but only the finest families could claim direct descent from gods, kings, and heroes. Although not strictly speaking a caste system, these inherited hierarchies and categories were oppressive for most. Since only the rich and powerful could afford the best funeral arrangements, even death wouldn't free the citizen from his state. But the Orphics introduced something radical into the social equation. By becoming an Orphic mystic and initiate, or at least by hiring one

*Translation by Ronnie Pontiac.

to entertain you for a while, by practicing purification or buying it, and including in the grave the expensive item recommended, any humble person could walk right by the fools drinking the water of forgetfulness and find him or herself seated next to a hero at the table of the god of the underworld.

Euripides (ca. 450 BCE), the great tragic playwright of ancient Greece, had something to say about the followers of Orpheus in his play *Hippolytus;* words he put into the mouth of Theseus the slayer of the Minotaur: "Boast all you want! Show off your vegetarian diet! Call Orpheus lord! Practice Bacchic rituals of ecstasy and revere your long winded scriptures! I'm on to you. I say to everyone: beware these men! Hiding shameful schemes they hunt their prey with holy books!"

Euripides portrays an example of the Orphic type in this play, first-prize winner at the competition of 428 BCE. Hippolytus is the son of a queen of the Amazons. He's devoted to the chaste goddess of the hunt Artemis; he's even taken a vow of chastity. Aphrodite takes offense at his neglect. In revenge, the goddess of love inspires his stepmother Phaedra to become so enamored with Hippolytus she starves herself hoping to at least die with her honor intact. Her desperate nurse suggests to Hippolytus that consummating the infatuation might cure Phaedra. In response Hippolytus delivers a tirade that details the evil of women and ends with a declaration of his hatred for them. Phaedra realizes that her only escape from Aphrodite's curse is to hang herself. Expressing Aphrodite's vindictive indignance, Phaedra leaves a note falsely accusing Hippolytus of raping her. His father Theseus believes his son tried to force himself on his stepmother. Everyone blames Hippolytus, even his own grandfather Poseidon who answers Theseus's vengeful prayer by causing a chariot accident that mangles the innocent young man. When Artemis explains the truth, Theseus is devastated. Hippolytus forgives his father with his last breath.

But why does Euripides have Theseus curse Hippolytus for calling Orpheus his lord? Hippolytus is not explicitly a member of the Orphic community, but he does have the Orphic attitude. Critical of his contemporaries, he's abstemious, which makes him part of a counterculture Euripides despises.

It's a seductive thing for scholars to find theories in scanty evidence, and some of the most important theories about Orphism originated when there were few artifacts to study. Much has been lost to fire, to vandalism, and all the other means of destruction at time's disposal, especially during the Dark Ages, when destroying pagan relics was considered virtuous.

Scholars have argued for centuries about the Orphics and their mysteries. Some imagined Orphism as a proto-Protestant religion, a virtuous reaction against extravagant idolatry of Olympian religious tradition with its colossal ivory and gold statue of Zeus and other celebrations of worldly power. Others followed Plato and Euripides, dismissing the Orphics as so many spiritual vagabonds hustling fake books said to be from the pen of Orpheus. From the sacred books of oracles, they chose the most vague that could fit many occasions. Offering entertainments as purifications, the binding of enemies, and initiations, they promised a better afterlife to gullible clients and provided guidance not only for the guilt ridden and the dying but also for the dead. Entire cities might hire such a service for a respected native who died without the necessary rituals to forgive unjust deeds.

Plutarch reports what happened when one such priest for hire approached a Spartan king. Spartans were renowned for their silence and for their snappy and brief comebacks. They were the insult comics of ancient Greece. So what did the Spartan king say to the underfed, raggedy, wandering Orphic priest who claimed he could confer initiations that would guarantee happiness after death? "What are you waiting for?" The same story is told with the Athenian philosopher Antisthenes the Cynic in the role of the Spartan king.

From the perspective of organized religions, then and now, such a disorganized spiritual practice could be dismissed as a collection of fakirs pretending to have spiritual authority. Yet wandering monks and priests have been known and respected in early Catholicism, Russian Orthodox Christianity, Hinduism, Buddhism, and other living traditions.

And what are we to make of the *teletai*? Nothing more than fake rituals peddled by frauds pretending to be religious experts? Were they rituals practiced by solitary mystics, or mysteries experienced by crowds of initiates? The famous hymns of Orpheus are really the *teletai* of Orpheus. *Hymns* isn't the ideal word to translate the ancient Greek word *teletai*. Ritual, initiation, marriage, bearing fruit in season, ripening fruit to perfection, magical potency, and finishing are all possible definitions.

Normandi Ellis has written eloquently about hieroglyphics as spells or affirmations. To carefully choose the right words, and to write them down in the correct way, is a kind of magical ritual in any language. Dr. Ellis points out the similar consonants of two words with very different origins: the ancient Egyptian *heka,* or spell, and the Japanese poetic form of haiku. Words selected precisely can have a magical effect.

The Derveni papyrus is an allegorical commentary on Orphic ideas from the time after Heraclitus and before Plato; it is also the earliest surviving book in Europe. It includes the striking image of the god Uranus ejaculating all the stars into the sky. The author considers himself an expert on esoteric matters, and he's quite intolerant of his less ethical and knowledgable competitors. As Radcliffe Edmonds writes: "the Derveni author denigrates, not the practice of *teletai,* the offering of sacrifices, or the consultation of oracles, but rather the inferior way in which others perform these religious acts" (2008, 32).

Chrysippus (ca. 280 BCE), the Stoic philosopher from Cilicia, east of Syria, defined *teletai* as writings about divine matters. Certainly a book can be a religious initiation, as the Bible, Qu'ran, and Bhagavad Gita prove.

In the twentieth century, the climate of scholarship changed. Christian agendas and the influence of growing up in Christian culture were carefully set aside from the process of assessing non-Christian cultures. New tools of scholarship allowed neutral examination of what had long been emotionally charged areas of study. Historians began to wonder if Orphism had ever really been a movement at all. The long list of allegedly Orphic relics and remains was dismantled and decommissioned until almost nothing remained. Pythagoreans had communities. Not Orphics. But then some pesky discoveries by archaeologists yet again undid the dominant narrative. The possibility of Orphic communities had to be admitted.

The Orphic battle in academia still rages with able champions on both sides. Alberto Bernabé makes a persuasive argument for restoring babies tossed out with the bathwater, and Edmonds is equally persuasive reminding us that however suggestive the evidence in certain contexts, examination of the individual parts reveals just how problematic it is to identify them as Orphic at all.

Edmonds writes "that Orphism was not a single unified Church, but is best understood as a collection of diverse counter-cultural religious movements whose major proponents were itinerant 'craftsmen' of purification who provided services for a wide variety of customers" (1999, 37).

There were ancient skeptics as well. "I would have known of any songs of Orpheus, if any there are," wrote Apollonius of Tyana, the Pythagorean philosopher who complained about being put in the same category as magi and Orphics. A pagan rival to Jesus, he allegedly stopped a riot with the dignity of his calm demeanor.

Orphic may have been a catch-all phrase in ancient Greece for anything neither Homeric nor Olympian. The phrase could be a generic category for a cluster of related interests, like New Age in our own culture. But no one can deny that the worldview had shifted from one where fragile humans who experienced suffering wondered which god or goddess they had offended to one where an immortal soul was caught in materiality, literally encased in a body. Aristotle may not have been an Orphic in much, but he was when he described the angst of soul in body to be like that of the Etruscan pirate torture of tying a captive face-to-face with a corpse. As we have seen, *soma sema* was a famous Orphic saying, the body a tomb, or cave, or prison, but *sema* also refers to a sign or a mark or, as Gregory Nagy called it, a "coded message." In Plato's *Cratylus,* Socrates guesses at the origin of the word for body, suggesting it may come from tomb or to imprison.

With the death of Orpheus at the hands of frenzied women, the Orphic myth draws a clear line of demarcation between past and future. In the past, we celebrated delirious ecstasy and the mania of possession in the rites of Dionysus, and we gladly sacrificed animals as part of our civic and religious duty, but now we understand that the sacrificed animal may have contained the soul of a human being once dear to us in another incarnation, and we also understand that madness can only lead to excess, as it did in the slaying of Orpheus.

A new more civilized vision of the mysteries of Dionysus was born. The religion of the hunters was transformed into the religion of citizens. Apollo could not be praised with blood and guts. Apollo, the symbol of purity and intellectual light, required a more refined spiritual practice. Oracles, music, philosophy, the use of reason to understand the world replaced atavistic frenzy in the forest.

Was the horror of killing dawning on a society that had celebrated warriors? Was there a collective realization that animal sacrifice and the opportunistic murder of fellow human beings might offend the gods? According to King Nestor in the *Iliad,* the golden age for the Homeric Greeks were the days when warriors greater than Achilles walked on Earth. The golden age as understood by Orpheus became instead a time when sacrificing animals was a sin and all human beings were vegetarians. When human souls can reincarnate as animals, eating any kind of meat becomes cannibalism.

In his book *On Abstinence from Animal Food,* Porphyry wrote about appropriate rituals for divine beings: "But for the gods of the sky, wandering and fixed, the sun their leader, and the moon next, we should kindle a flame, which is like them, and do what the theologian says. Not one living creature should be sacrificed, offer instead honey, barley, and the fruits of the soil including flowers." The "theologian" is Orpheus.

The Orphic Mysteries

As we have seen, important scholars have argued that Orphism was more literary movement than organized religion. But Plutarch, the great pagan biographer of the first century CE, called himself an initiate of the Orphic mysteries. He didn't agree with every aspect of them. He thought the warning about horrific hells awaiting the unjust was vulgar, and he thought morbid the constant self-examination and self-denial of the Orphic way of life. Yet he reported the consolation the mysteries gave him and his wife when facing life's most difficult challenges.

Plutarch describes his experience of the mysteries as "nervous journeys" in the dark, exhausted running here and there, until "shivering and trembling," having found no way out and facing death, a "marvelous light" meets you and you're welcomed into meadows and open country, where people dance and sing of holy things. When Plutarch wrote of "sacred visions," many scholars argue that the great biographer was tripping. The Eleusinian mysteries included drinking *kykeon,* a psychoactive brew. Others believe sophisticated machinery helped create theatrical presentations that may or may not have been understood to be dramatizations, rather than manifestations or hallucinations.

We don't know what took place in the Orphic rites. Speculation is all we have. Initiation may have started with a long wait in a torchlit cavern with walls painted to show all the suffering of life, from realistic portrayals of wounds and diseases to the ravages of age and natural disasters. For people who had no screens to flood their worlds with such imagery, who had only their personal experiences, or lack of experience, to go by, these must have been startling scenes. The message was, as Dionysus enthusiast Jim Morrison put it a couple thousand years later, "no one in here gets out alive."

Thronosis was a part of the initiation process, according to some scholars, but what exactly was it? As with so much of ancient Greek culture, the answer depends on which city-state you're asking about. In the Eleusinian mysteries, it's likely the initiation began with a long sit on a stool with a death shroud over your head, as Demeter was said to have sat in sorrow on a stool after the news of Persephone's abduction. In solemn silence contemplate mortality and mourn for your lost ones, for yourself, for the whole sick sad world, perhaps?

Meanwhile in the Korybantic mysteries, men with chalk on their faces, warriors dressed as Titans, danced in a frenzy around the candidate for initiation who must have endured a terrifying few moments wondering just how far the reenactment of the dismembering of Dionysus was going to go. Rumors of cannibalism among the mad followers of the god of Mount Nysa must have left some aspiring initiates wondering if they were going to wind up that night's entree.

Jane Harrison, the first professional scholar of the female gender in the United Kingdom, argued that a wheel was involved in the Orphic mysteries. The German scholar Dr. Eisler agreed. He tried to prove that Christ on the cross had actually been inspired by the use of a wheel in the Orphic mysteries. Initiates, he suggested, may have been tied to a wheel and spun so they could feel the dizzy helplessness of repeated reincarnation in helpless ignorance. But these scenarios are widely considered flights of fancy, not scholarship. The current compromise vision of what Orphism might have been no longer includes the Orphic mysteries as a religious institution. Instead, we have something closer to the New England transcendentalists, or the Elizabethan intellectuals, or the Pythagoreans. And yet evidence from ca. 500 BCE proves private mysteries were being practiced apart from organized religion, though we have no details.

Today, the theorem and *tetractys* of Pythagoras are remembered more than the way of life he taught or his philosophy of numbers. He was a revered teacher, a man who gave the world crucial first steps in science, geometry, music, higher mathematics, philosophy, and religion.

Pythagoras founded the Pythagorean brotherhood, which devoted itself to the study of mathematics. As is the case so often in history, only the upper class had the leisure to devotedly study this new way of seeing the world, so the brotherhood was an aristocratic affair. Their fellow citizens were intrigued by the faultless ethics and enlightening ideas of these visionaries, so they were invited into politics where they were embraced as reformers.

But the early Pythagoreans were attacked ca. 500 BCE by Cylon, a local noble who was so infuriated by the brotherhood's rejection of him that he tried to kill them all. Some say that's when Pythagoras died. Another version of his death is by suicide in exile. Iamblichus—the great Neoplatonist, and an inspiration to generations of occultists, in his *Life of Pythagoras,* which can also be translated as *The Pythagorean Way of Life*—dismisses the attack by Cylon as a minor event greatly exaggerated. Pythagoras, he says, returned home and the society flourished. Did the myth of Orpheus become confused with his follower Pythagoras, so Pythagoras was said to have died at the hands of irate enemies?

Pythagorean practices were hardly radical from the twenty-first-century point of view. One that people today might find useful is the Pythagorean recollection: reflect on the events of the day, while relaxing quietly just before sleep. By going backward moment by moment, examining what could have been done differently, how better outcomes could have been achieved, any life can be improved.

No scholar can miss the similarities between the beliefs of the Pythagoreans and the Orphics. Both forbade the sacrifice of animals and detested meat eating, although not all Pythagoreans were vegetarians. Both taught nonviolence and the importance of purity when facing the afterlife. Both used music to illustrate abstract philosophical and mathematical concepts. Both may have taught reincarnation, although we are more confident that Pythagoras did. Aristotle in his book *On the Soul* tells us that some Orphics believed the soul to be independent of the body. With that and a few lines by Theophrastus, the successor of Aristotle, generations of scholars have argued that belief in reincarnation was an important feature of Orphism. What else could the painful cycle, or wheel of deep grief, mentioned in Orphic writings be? But, of course, it could mean life in this world of the lunar cycle, of tides, the wheel of day and night, of seasons, cause and effect, and all the other circles that dominate the living.

Chios (ca. 450 BCE)—the friend of Aeschylus (whom Cicero called a Pythagorean) and a rival of Euripides in Athens—was the author of a Pythagorean text. His blunt opinion was that: "Pythagoras wrote some poems and signed them as Orpheus." Later writers provided names of Italian Pythagoreans who were identified as authors of specific books attributed to Orpheus. Was this a long-standing oral tradition finally committed to writing, or a spurious invention, or a combination of both? Perhaps Pythagoreans wrote poems about cosmology and the meaning of life and signed them "Orpheus" in imitation of the Egyptian scribes who never signed their own names, only the name of Thoth, god of scribes.

Timing is everything when it comes to a new means of distribution. Elvis became a superstar partly because he arrived at the right moment to take advantage of the fact that the then generation of teenagers had, for the first time, record players they could use in the privacy of their bedrooms. Orpheus was the Elvis of books, back when books were the new thing in ancient Greece. As Edmonds wrote: "The literate initiates of Orphism became the champions of books but at the same time rejected the world, setting up for themselves a secret library that revolved around Orpheus' unique voice" (2013, 103).

By signing the name of Orpheus to their own books, these ancient authors claimed for their words the direct authority of someone whose ideas about the gods were deep, pure, and holy. To bring up Orpheus when praising justice was acceptable in the courts of classical Athens, as we read in the speech against Aristogiton by the great Athenian orator Demosthenes. After all, Orpheus was said to have been the founder of many mysteries throughout Greece, including the most sacred, the Eleusinian.

Proclus, the last of the Neoplatonic philosophers, wrote, during the time of the fall of the Western Roman Empire, that *the body, a tomb* is not only Orphic but also Pythagorean. But he claims that Pythagoras did not learn the divine secrets from Orpheus but from Aglaothemis, the teacher of Orpheus, about whom almost nothing is known. "What Orpheus expressed mystically using ancient folk tales," Proclus wrote, "Pythagoras learned when he celebrated the mysteries in Thrace."

But according to Proclus, Aglaothemis was not the only teacher Orpheus had. Proclus adds that Orpheus learned the doctrine and the divine mysteries from his mother, Calliope, the muse of eloquence and of epic poetry. Mnemosyne, or Memory, is Calliope's mother and therefore the grandmother of Orpheus. Other versions of the myth have Apollo teaching Orpheus. Orpheus was also thought to have learned the sacred mysteries from Persephone, who took his right hand in hers when he met the goddess in Hades. Comic book and multimedia storyteller Neil Gaiman referred to this in his 2015 poem "Orphee." "When Orpheus was young he got the girl back from Hell safely. That's where the years came from. Euridice comes home from Hell and the flowers bloom and the world puddles and quickens, and it's Spring." In this stanza he deliberately conflates Eurydice and Persephone.

Like the other great literary and artistic movements of Western civilization, this alleged Pythagorean literary circle set out to change the way its readers viewed the quality and meaning of life. What the members of this circle didn't expect was the rise of a class of itinerant priests using their books, and forgeries aplenty, to sell rituals and charms to wealthy widows and anxious old men who never had the time to lead the philosophical life.

The Athenians, who still prized their oral histories, were suspicious of this literate elite who turned up their noses at ambition and excitement, preparing themselves for death before they died. Why, they refused to eat meat!

But where did Pythagoras get his education? From an obscure Thracian mystic? Was he a spontaneous genius? Herodotus (ca. 450 BCE) says succinctly that the Orphic and Bacchic mysteries were actually Pythagorean, which is to say Egyptian. The

Egyptian Book of the Dead certainly resembles in tone and content the fragments we have from the Orphic golden leaves. In both cases, the living would read the texts and bury them with the dead. Writing not much later, the Athenian master of rhetoric Isocrates (ca. 400 BCE) agrees that the Pythagoreans were inspired by Egyptian religious beliefs.

So were the Orphics and the Orphic mysteries the invention of the Pythagoreans? Bernabé has compared Orphic studies to Penelope weaving daily only to undo her work every night. No simple answers can be depended on when studying Orpheus. For example, as we have seen, Herodotus said Pythagoras created the Orphic mysteries. But Iamblichus insists: "Pythagoras was taught by the disciples of Orpheus."

Attic vase painters portrayed Orpheus as a civilized Greek charming spear-wielding Thracian outlanders in their gaudy embroidered cloaks and pointy fox-skin caps. Thrace and Macedonia were the highlands of ancient Greece. Thracians originated the worship of Ares, god of war, Artemis, the quick slaying huntress, and Dionysus, god of wine.

Wine was usually watered down but was undiluted when used during the sacred mysteries, to intoxicate and liberate as the liquor of immortality. It allowed the initiate to regain consciousness outside the limitations of the body and daily habits. The wine, as the juice of the grape, was the blood of Dionysus, god of the grape vines. A drink of immortality was given by Osiris in the ancient Egyptian mysteries. But as suits a country with a hot climate surrounded by desert, the magical liquid was water.

The Thracians wore their hair long and decorated themselves with tattoos. They loved drinking, music, and dancing. They set out food for sea eagles. They bred, trained, and rode horses so well they might be the source for the myth of the half-man, half-horse centaurs. Thracian women were fierce warriors, possibly the source of the Amazon myth. Thracian men were legendary for marching into battle drunk. Snowy Thrace was known as the Land of Prophets. Spartacus was Thracian.

Today in Bulgaria, in the area that was once Thrace, Orpheus has a statue, his lyre appears on many signs, streets are named after him, along with restaurants and resorts. He even has a tomb. The local archaeologists claim him as a Thracian king, ca. 2000 BCE, who was killed before he could accomplish his goal of bringing peace to warring tribes. It's intriguing that Egyptian scarab beetle charms were found in Thracian ruins.

But then the Athenians claimed that they hosted the first Orphic mysteries. And then there's Crete, hardly considered Greek by many ancient Greeks, with their outlandish bare-breasted women and young people showing off by leaping over the horns of charging bulls like Olympic gymnasts. In Crete, Orpheus was sometimes depicted with the head of a bird, playing his lyre, attracting birds from the sky. "Clothed all in white I flee mortal birth and avoiding the place of corpses I guard myself against eating ensouled flesh," Euripides had his chorus of mystics from Crete sing, sounding quite Orphic.

Diodorus of Sicily writes that the mysteries may have begun in Crete, or reached Greece from there: "the rites of initiation celebrated by Athenians in Eleusis, the most famous of them, and those of Samothrace, and the rites in Thrace among the Cicones, which Orpheus introduced, are all in the form of a mystery. But in the city of Knossos on the island of Crete the custom from ancient times is that initiation is freely given to everyone." Of course, that doesn't mean the mysteries in Crete couldn't have been inspired by the Egyptians. Diodorus wrote that "Orpheus traveled to Egypt to understand their traditions regarding death, he invented myths about the underworld, borrowing some things and making up others."*

Diodorus also claimed that Orpheus studied magic with the Dactyls, a mythic race of prophets who discovered how to work with metals. When they arrived in Samothrace, they frightened the locals with their spells and mysteries. They were the founders of *goetia,* a way of singing that bridges the worlds of the living and the dead. The term, much later, in the underbelly of Christianity, became associated with grimoires concerned with ritual evocations of angels and demons. A dactyl was said to have founded the Olympic Games. Did they represent a people otherwise forgotten to history?

But the argument for ancient Egypt is not yet complete. The *Orphic Argonautica,* the story of Jason and the Argonauts, is told with Orpheus as the lead character. How is Orpheus depicted in the story? He knows how to interpret the signs sent by the gods. He knows which deity must be appeased. A storm that prevents the ship from sailing requires a ritual for the goddess Rhea. An earthquake indicates the footsteps of Apollo, who demands an altar be built. To get the Argo home safely, Orpheus performs rituals for the local deities, explaining the presence of foreign deities in the Orphic hymns. In this tale Orpheus himself claims to have visited Memphis and the other sacred cities of Egypt.

History provides a more complicated picture. When Greek mercenaries first settled in the Nile Delta, the Egyptians provided interpreters, but it seems unlikely that the Greeks who considered the Egyptians barbarians, and the Egyptians who guarded their spiritual mysteries from the profane, would be sharing detailed information about Egyptian mortuary practices and afterlife beliefs. But it may have happened, as a Greek mercenary's grave was found and all the details of burial were traditionally Egyptian.

---

*Translation by Ronnie Pontiac.

Also, sages have been known to go with armies to foreign lands for the purpose of learning.

The similarities between the Orphic and Egyptian beliefs are striking. The Egyptians had a tree in the afterlife, but theirs was a sycamore, instead of the Orphic cypress. *Nehat,* the ancient Egyptian word for sycamore, meant "shelter." The newly dead arrived thirsty and begging for water in the beliefs of both cultures. The *Egyptian Book of the Dead* included a formula to help the dead remember their names. A declaration of purity was important in both. And like the Orphic golden leaves, copies of the *Book of the Dead* were buried with those who could afford them. Some have even speculated that Orpheus, torn apart by maenads, whose head floats away to become an oracle, is merely a garbled or refashioned version of Osiris who was also torn apart. Perhaps the Greeks were uncomfortable with the Egyptian fascination with the phallus of Osiris, early scholars wondered, and replaced it with a more socially acceptable decapitated head.

But the similarities between Orphic beliefs is even more striking when compared with "Great voyage of the soul," a Hittite text. For example, both involve a choice between a path of remembering or forgetting. The Orphic fountain of forgetfulness suggests the Hittite sea of forgetfulness. For both, punishment involves the soul mired in mud. In both myths, a young deity is torn apart. In both, the soul is given a drink that restores divinity.

Butterworth in his obscure classic *The Tree at the Navel of the Earth* shared his provocative theory that the *Odyssey* records the Homeric reaction to the invasion of Eastern mysticism. The cyclops satirizes the third eye of the cave-dwelling sages who renounced life among mortals. The lotus eaters represent irresponsible cults who practiced spiritual ecstasy, like the Orphics. And wicked Circe was a teacher of sexual mysteries as well as a witch who turned men into pigs. Odysseus representing the good old-fashioned Olympian ideal outsmarts them all because, ultimately, his way of life is life affirming, while theirs turns away from life as they prepare themselves for the supposedly greater rewards of death.

Experts on ancient music wonder if Orpheus performed chromatic scales and quarter tones, a lute more like a sitar in sound. The parallels between the Orphic path and the yogic are articulated by Joseph Campbell: "a system both of thought and practice, exactly paralleling that of Indian asceticism, was communicated by initiated masters to little circles of devotees" (1964, 183).

Was Madame Blavatsky right after all? Was Orpheus a missionary from India as she insisted? Did the Vedic tradition directly influence Orphism? Campbell doubts it. "More likely is a common source in the archaic Bronze Age order, which in its last phases underwent the negative transformation that I have termed *The Great Reversal,* when a literature of lament arose from Egypt to Mesopotamia, following centuries of invasion, murder, and rapine" (1964, 184).

With so many potential origins we can't discern which one is the historical truth. But we can appreciate that the Orphic impulse was not outside the current of cultures all around the Mediterranean. Whatever the difference in names and other details, the themes of memory and forgetting, of necessary purification, and of attained immortality were the same.

The Golden Leaves

Life Death Life
Truth

As we have seen, those words were found inscribed on a bone tablet. While no gold leaf, it has been included for consideration among the few possible remnants of Orphic funeral practices. Many of the gold leaves were found in Crete, but this Orphic relic survived near the Black Sea, in what we now call Ukraine, in a grave not far from an ancient temple of Apollo. Gold leaves have been found in graves from southern Italy to Macedonia, most dating from the fourth and fifth centuries BCE, around the time of Plato and Aristotle.

What are these gold leaf objects? Leaf in the sense of gold foil, but a few are cut to look like leaves. Historians usually call them gold tablets, though they are very small and thin. German scholars adopted the term *totenpass,* meaning a passport for the dead. One gold leaf's message starts with the word *password*.

The gold tablet, found in a woman's otherwise undistinguished grave in a large necropolis near Hipponion in Southern Italy, provided a less cryptic message:

Here is the password of Memory. When you die
you go to the vast halls of Hades. A spring is on your
    right,
and by it stands a shining cypress tree
where the descending souls of the dead refresh
    themselves.
Stay away from that spring!
Further on you'll find refreshing water
flowing from the lake of Memory.
Guardians stand by.
They will ask you sharply
what you seek in the dank shadows of Hades.
Say: "I am a child of earth and starry heaven
and I'm parched with thirst. Now give me
refreshing water to drink from the lake of Memory."
They'll speak to the king of the underworld,
then they'll give you to drink from the lake of
    Memory,
and you, having drunk, will go along the holy road
initiates and mystics travel.*

As we have seen Orphism remains stubbornly mysterious. A place where even skilled researchers end up chasing their own shadows, a fertile breeding ground for mystics and magicians.

For example, a phrase that appears on the gold tablets is "a kid, I have rushed to the milk and fallen in." This has inspired much poetic reverie. Among scholars the assumption was that this was probably ancient slang for really finding yourself in your element, like a "donkey in hay." Some, perhaps influenced by the Neoplatonists, imagined a deeper symbol in the idea of a young

*Translation by Ronnie Pontiac.

58

goat drowning in milk. Could this be a metaphor for the way the soul loses consciousness when imprisoned in a material body? What might have nourished us instead smothers us.

Professor Martin Nilsson in the mid-twentieth century thought the reference to milk an adaptation of a popular proverb of the time, meaning simply abundance and happiness. In the twenty-first century scholars Sarah Iles Johnson and Fritz Graf agreed that milk symbolized the beginning of a more abundant life.

Or perhaps the kid in milk is a symbol for the newly liberated soul rushing to the milk of spiritual sustenance. Recently Stian Torjussen has argued that the milk mentioned in the gold tablets is a symbol of immortality. He points out that in Greece since the seventh century BCE milk and stars have been connected. The queen of the gods, Hera, was said to have created the stars when she sprayed milk across the sky, and to this day we call our galaxy the Milky Way. The kid jumping into the milk must be of the race of starry heaven.

A kid in milk is covered in white, like the white shroud of the dead or the white robe of the Orphic, which may have been one and the same. A kid in milk could also be an image of a newborn encased in the amniotic sac. All are symbols of the spiritual rebirth of the initiate.

Then another gold tablet was found in which a bull rushes to milk and falls in. That's an unnatural image. Bulls don't drink milk. Bulls are symbols of Dionysus. Finally, the word *milk* itself came into question. The word could also be interpreted as referring to the froth of sea-foam. In some variations of the Dionysus myth, he is a bull that charges off a cliff into the frothing white sea-foam. Could the gold tablet actually be referring to that ancient myth?

To further complicate matters, in ancient Greek religion hymns commonly invite gods to leap into the milk, into the wine, into the youth maturing that year. The kid or bull leaping into milk might be nothing more than a springtime prayer.

Edmonds makes a strong argument that the golden tablets were inscribed with sentences from an oracle. The earliest records never mention Orpheus as having visited the underworld, and he's not listed among those with special knowledge of the afterlife. His fame, according to them, is for his rites of purification and his oracles. Someone could have asked the oracle of Orpheus about crossing over to the afterlife and received the famous answer in hexameters about the glowing cypress tree and avoiding the waters of forgetfulness, including what to say to the guardians of the water of memory—that you are a child of earth and starry heaven but of the race of heaven.

Another gold leaf promises that though once mortal the initiate is now a god. But no other leaf says that. Edmonds suggests that the "child of earth and starry heaven" phrase is a reference to "the ancestral heroes, the founders of the race who lived in closer conjunction with the gods than the ordinary folk today" (2010, 111), races like the Tritopatores (Thrice Fathers) from the times when gods feasted among men. On the other hand, the phrase may simply be a reference to Memory's parents, Gaia the earth and Ouranos the starry sky god.

Except for those golden leaves that share the same content, how do we know that any of the golden leaves were connected by a consistent belief system or community? Once thought to have been the symbols of exclusive membership in a mystical cult, they are now considered at best instructions for ritual dances or motions, at worst the relics of unscrupulous traveling oracle mongers. The small number of them makes them seem rare, and their influence therefore appears to have been relatively minor, but it's easy to speculate that gold attracts grave robbers, and most of the tablets may have been stolen and melted down long ago.

The Night Gathering

Perhaps the most important gossip in history is Plato. Some have argued that he was a Pythagorean or an Orphic himself. The Neoplatonist Olympiodorus the Younger wrote: "Plato paraphrases Orpheus everywhere." Proclus wrote in his *Platonic Theology* that Greek religious doctrines came from the Orphic mysteries.

Under the pressures of materialism on one hand, and their Christian faith on the other, several generations of scholars set up Plato as a creative genius, considering his writings a foundation of Western civilization. The Neoplatonists, who insisted that to understand Plato one must understand Orpheus and Pythagoras, were ignored. Influential scholars dismissed the Orphic literature and its influence as an irrational intrusion into Greek culture. But more recent scholarship has shown that the Neoplatonists and their admirers, including Marsilio Ficino, Thomas Taylor, Madame Blavatsky, Thomas Johnson, Alexander Wilder, and Manly Palmer Hall, may have had it right.

With his emphasis on how music can contribute to the greatness or the demise of a civilization and his meticulous analysis of how citizens should behave, Plato may not have been a

Pythagorean, but he was certainly inspired by them, and like them he drew spiritual inspiration from the laws governing numbers and motion.

In the "Myth of Er," from Plato's *Republic,* the afterlife Plato describes has Orphic and Pythagorean overtones. Plato sneers at the foolish souls who, when it comes time to choose their reincarnations, only look for the most dazzling fates written on the shards of destiny; they never think to look at the back of each to see what corresponding suffering is written there. Only Odysseus, the ultimate symbol of ancient Greek ingenuity, searches for and chooses the shard no one wants: a quiet life with little suffering.

Orphic and Pythagorean concepts and practices are woven throughout the Platonic dialogues. But Plato is no fan of Orpheus and the Orphics. He dismisses the Orphics as hustlers peddling fake books to rich clients. Why did Plato dismiss Orpheus as a coward, adding that it suited his profession of musician? (Also, was this the first recorded musician joke in Western history?) Plato believed that Orpheus should have died to be with his beloved instead of making so much fuss the offended gods punished him by showing him only an apparition of his wife and then taking it away, finally sending the maenads to tear him limb from limb. Plato says that afterward Orpheus so hated women he chose to be reborn as a motherless swan.

Yet, Plato mentions Orpheus in ten of his dialogues. In the *Apology* Socrates lists Orpheus as the first of the four greats he is eager to meet in the afterlife. He mentions the sweet voice and sweet hymns of Orpheus. He ranks Orpheus with the great inventors in *Laws* but not for music. What then did Orpheus invent? Perhaps the hexameter form that revolutionized Greek poetry.

In Plato's *Laws* three old men discuss how to organize Crete's new colony. Plato's choice of leadership inspired some scholars to argue that when he wrote it he must have been senile. The leaders of Plato's ideal community were a small circle of Orphic priests, or priests of Apollo, who would decide which laws to keep, to change, or to repeal. If new laws were needed, they would make them. Plato named them the Night Gathering. Their meetings were brief, from the earliest light of dawn until sunrise revealed the perfect circle of the sun. Plato knew that Orpheus had chosen that time for his morning worship of Apollo.

Orphic and Pythagorean connections to Crete inspired some scholars to speculate as to whether *Laws* is a fictionalized portrait of one of the Pythagorean communities Plato visited in his youth. But scholars have shunned his foreshadowing of the magic and mysticism of Neoplatonism in Book Ten, where he argues that the soul creates the body, not the other way around. Consciousness is not the effervescence of brains and nervous systems. The intelligence of consciousness created them and everything else in the physical world. For modern Platonic scholars who view *Laws* as the beginning of political science and social studies, the presence of these Orphic themes has been problematic.

Ignorant or uninterested in Plato's insistence that the Greek myths must be understood as analogies and allegories, early Christian writers busily undermining paganism often quoted ancient Greek myths as illustrations of pagan barbarity. Not only were the gods said to engage in obscene fornication and incest, the stories also included tales of child murder and cannibalism. Of course, they never mentioned that the Old Testament could give the Olympians a run for their money. Neither did they mention that their own religion was built around a human sacrifice and a sacred ritual that involved the symbolic cannibalism of a savior's blood and body.

Dio Chrystostom wrote ca. 100 CE that human beings arose

from the blood of the Titans. Because the Titans hate the gods and attacked them, the gods don't care for us. The gods punished the Titans by incarcerating them in Tartarus. They punish us by imprisoning us in bodies. Death means the sentence has been served.

Though Plutarch in his essay "On Eating Meat" calls ancient the myth of Dionysus torn apart by the Titans, nowhere does he say that humanity was born from the ashes. By explaining why he thinks vegetarianism is a superior spiritual path, Plutarch may also reveal the reason for the Orphic prohibition against meat eating. He writes that meat obscures the soul. It makes the body too heavy for the soul, blocking out the light with excess density. Instead of being an effortless vehicle for the soul, the body becomes an affliction, distracting the soul with forgetfulness, dragging it down to the level of the Titans where destruction follows every action.

Clement of Alexandria (ca. 200 CE), a Christian Platonist, referred to verses from Orpheus about the Titans using the Seven Toys to lure the baby Dionysus to his doom: "a knucklebone, hoop, apples, spinner, looking-glass, tuft of wool" (Edmonds 2008). Neoplatonists and other metaphysically inclined writers argued that this is a symbol of how the soul is lured by the fascinating elements, compounds, planets, and other aspects of the material world and is then torn apart to create, govern, and sustain the various organs and other parts of the body. For them the apples of the Titans were the planets that weave the fates of incarnate souls.

Orpheus remained an important influence on subsequent pagan Greek culture. The following quote attributed to Ptolemy, the famous second-century astrologer, astronomer, geographer, and mathematician of Alexandria, is reminiscent of the Orphic formula: "I am a child of earth and starry heaven, but my race is of heaven."

> I know I was born mortal, a creature of a day.
> But when in my mind I trace the revolving spirals of
>   the stars,
> My feet touch earth no more, with Zeus I feast,
> Ambrosia fed, nourished alongside the gods.*

In the third century CE Artemidorus, a soothsayer, wrote a once famous book about dream interpretation called *Oneirocritica*. He lived in Ephesus not far from the area in what is now Turkey that most likely produced the Orphic hymns. He tells his readers that dreams of "choruses and hymn-singing mean deception and deceit—keep in mind that it makes no difference whether a person dreams that he himself does any of these things, or is present while they are being done" (Artemidorus tr. 2012). Evidently, he shared Plato's low opinion of "priests" pedaling Orphic products like door-to-door salesmen.

To dream of Dionysus is lucky for a farmer but bad news for a sailor. "Dancing to honor Dionysus, waving the sacred wand, carrying trees in procession, or doing anything else pleasing to the god is inauspicious for all men but slaves. For most it foretells foolishness and harm because of the bewilderment of the mental processes by frenzy, but for slaves it symbolizes freedom" (Artemidorus tr. 2012).

Later, Artemidorus tells this strange story about a dream of Dionysus: "A woman dreamed she was drunk dancing in a chorus to honor Dionysus. Three years later she killed her own child"

---

*Translation by Ronnie Pontiac.

(tr. 2012). Artemidorus adds that the feast of Dionysus is every third year and that another mother, Agave, frenzied by her worship of Dionysus, famously ripped her son Pentheus apart. In this way the woman's dream foreshadowed her fate, Artemidorus explains.

The twilight of paganism was presided over by the Neoplatonic school of philosophers. Orpheus was especially important to the Neoplatonists because he was somewhat acceptable to their Christian rivals. Orpheus was a way for pagan writers to claim that they had a Jesus before Jesus. It became a Neoplatonic pre-occupation to go back through the works of Aristotle and Plato making comments in the margins meant to illuminate hidden meanings. As Sara Rappe (2000, 143) wrote: "Orpheus, from the enchanted visionary of the earlier tradition, becomes a metaphysically astute theologian for the later Neoplatonists."

Proclus is little remembered these days, though a swarm of academic studies about his works have been published recently. He was a great influence on not just medieval European philosophy and mysticism but also Islamic. Proclus believed that Orpheus, Homer, and Hesiod drew wisdom from the same well, from teachings that Pythagoras and Plato explained.

Proclus gave us a modified version of the Orphic creation myth in the *Orphic Rhapsody*. In the beginning was eternity, undecaying time, and a force, call it necessity or compulsion. As eternity and necessity wound around each other they evolved aether, the organizing force, and chaos, the primal emptiness. These two combined to create a cosmic egg that spun faster and faster until Phanes burst out in radiance and harmony, manifesting light waves and sound waves, the first being. The only one to witness him was his sister-daughter-wife, Night. Depending on one's opinion of the Neoplatonists this can be understood as a crude pagan incest myth or a way of conveying complex relationships between energies using only images. Many more steps of creation remained, including the entirety of creation waiting in Zeus's belly, the ultimate male usurpation of female creative power.

The Neoplatonists respected every detail of the creation they were trying to understand. Like Dionysus, they pointed out, Orpheus is torn into seven pieces, indicating the seven musical notes and the seven then known planets; therefore, seven is a holy number, and categories of sevens should be listed.

Marinus of Neapolis (ca. 475 CE), the biographer of Proclus, recalled studying the hymns of Orpheus with Proclus. Proclus shared with him the commentaries of Iamblichus and Syrianus on their interpretation. Marinus was so impressed he asked Proclus to put them in a book. But Proclus said he had a dream in which his teacher Syrianus forbade him to put the interpretations into writing.

Marinus also reports that when Proclus was on his deathbed, patiently suffering the pains of his final illness, he asked his friends to sing the hymns of Orpheus. Marinus said the hymns stopped the pain and brought Proclus serenity. At the very end, delirious, lapsing in and out of consciousness, unable to recognize his friends, Proclus would join in when the hymns were being sung, still able to remember the words.

Olympiodorus was the last pagan to lead the Platonic school in Alexandria. After his death, it passed into Christian hands and was moved to Constantinople. Was Olympiodorus an alchemist? Brisson has argued that Olympiodorus may have been sharing an alchemical allegory in his telling of the myth of Zeus burning the Titans and of the particles of smoke that are the material from which men were born. Was Olympiodorus describing an alchemical distillation process?

In 529 CE the Christian emperor Justinian I closed the Platonic school in Athens, where Plato and Aristotle had walked together, and the Byzantine Empire went about becoming infamous for the bureaucracy that would make its name an adjective for tortured and pointless complexity. Over the next several centuries, Christianity's reduction of the old gods to demons resulted in one of the most horrific acts of vandalism in history. Statues, temples, sacred groves, books, frescoes, and altars were destroyed or defaced. After the conversion of pagan temples to churches in Athens, which began with destructive mobs of overzealous Christians—singing hymns and laughing as they defaced masterpieces of the millennia—one Athenian philosopher dreamed of homeless Athena begging for shelter at his door.

A long lost great work of Neoplatonism has tempted the imaginations of metaphysicians for generations: *On the Agreement between Orpheus, Pythagoras, Plato and the Chaldean Oracles.* Many have argued that Neoplatonism, as the last statement of a proud pagan tradition that knew it was nearing the end, revealed secret doctrines for fear they would be lost forever. Christianity resembles Neoplatonism, these scholars argue, because it borrowed so much from the pagan mysteries. Or as Saint Basil the Great wrote ca. 360 CE: "So we, if wise, shall take from heathen books whatever befits us and is allied to the truth, and shall pass over the rest."

Today, most historians agree that the Neoplatonists were imposing the complexities of their own metaphysics onto cobbled-together myths and philosophical concepts. But there remains an enticing middle ground: because in all such matters words tend to be as much hindrance as help, it is possible that, while they may not have been mindful of scientific method, the Neoplatonists were pointing at truths that were essential to the more elevated pagan communities. Their rough and ready handling of time and place as they drew their examples may be somewhat offset by their constant reminders to readers that they are using a patchwork of images, myths, metaphors, and science to convey something that words cannot really capture.

For the Jews of ancient Alexandria, Orpheus was a monotheist who had studied under Moses. For the fresco painters of Roman catacombs, Orpheus was the prototype of Jesus the Good Shepherd. Gradually, the docile wild animals enchanted by the music of Orpheus were replaced with Jesus and a flock of domesticated sheep. Orpheus and Jesus both became popular symbols of the psychopomp that leads souls away from this life.

Orpheus on the mountaintop singing to dawn was compared to the Sermon on the Mount. The Easter egg could be the Orphic egg. A hematite magic amulet (ca. 350 CE), once in the collection of the Berlin Museum, depicted a man crucified on a cross with a moon and seven stars above his head and the words *Orpheos Bakkikoc*. It's now thought to be a forgery but was destroyed during World War II so the mystery remains.

The *Testament of Orpheus* was considered the most important Orphic document for six centuries after its "discovery" in ca. 300 CE. In it Orpheus, when in Egypt, met Moses who taught him about monotheism. Now an old man, Orpheus urges pagans to give up their pantheon and accept the one true God. It appears to be a forgery by a Jewish writer living in Alexandria, but generations of early Christian scholars never thought it too convenient to be genuine.

In 1150 Ioannes Galenos was a deacon with some surprising ideas, for example that Hercules and Jesus represent the same deity. In his study of Hesiod, the great poet who had lived almost two thousand years before the deacon, Galenos mentions the hymns of Orpheus. That's the earliest reference to them. But another flavor of the Orpheus myth was already developing: the prototype of the courtly lover. Orpheus was an inspiration to the culture of wandering troubadours of the High Middle Ages.

Around 1300 CE, Orpheus, though only named once in *The Divine Comedy,* was placed by Dante in "the philosophic family," those pagans who couldn't be saved since they lived before Jesus but who lived lives and taught beliefs that foreshadowed the Christian revelation. God provided a nice field for them off to the side where they could enjoy something like a pagan heaven. Orphic themes are woven throughout Dante's masterpiece. From weeping Filippo Argenti pulled down by wrathful hands to Francesca da Rimini whose predicament, speech, and character are practically a tribute to Virgil's portrait of Orpheus.

By ca. 1350, a popular book by a Benedictine monk moralizing on Ovid identified Jesus with Orpheus. Fifty years later an anonymous Franciscan, also writing about Ovid, wrote: "Orpheus clearly denotes Jesus Christ, Divine Word, the teacher of good doctrine." But a new Orpheus was already being born: the dashing knight, skillful musician, and romantic hero, Sir Orfeo. This Orpheus had less to do with Jesus and was compared instead to King David. But the Orphic hymns themselves, which had long been lost to historians, were about to make a dramatic reappearance.

Orpheus in the Renaissance

In 1462, at twenty-nine years of age, Marsilio Ficino had found his calling. He wished to live the contemplative life, translating Orpheus, Plato, the *Hermetica,* Plotinus, Iamblichus, Proclus, and Dionysius the Areopagite, exploring for himself, and sharing with others, the wonders and profundities of long forgotten pagan wisdom. But how? To live such a life would require the support of a wealthy patron.

Ficino decided to celebrate an Orphic ritual as a way of asking the universe to help him. While he was performing the *Hymn to the Cosmos* his father brought him letters from Cosimo de Medici, the ruler of the Republic of Florence. Cosimo wrote: "Yesterday I arrived at my Careggi estate, to cultivate not this place, but my mind. Join us, Marsilio, as soon as you can. Bring Plato's book on The Highest Good, which I expect you have translated from Greek to Latin as you said you would. What I want with all my heart is to know which way leads most certainly to happiness. Farewell. Join us, and bring your Orphic lyre" (Ungers 2008, 12).

Cosimo had awarded Ficino a villa in Careggi and income from a nearby farm so that he could devote himself to his transla-tions. Ficino wrote back to Cosimo that this serendipity "evoked in me the most immense wonder." Identifying himself with Orpheus, he displayed his belief that with an understanding of the harmonies underlying all creation, by tuning to the laws of life, a human being could change fate.

Ficino played his lyre, which had Orpheus painted on it, many times for friends, singing the Orphic hymns. His friends nicknamed him Orpheus. With Cosimo, Ficino founded the revived Platonic Academy in Florence, a place where great artists and humanists gathered to inspire one another. Cosimo's grandson, Lorenzo de' Medici, known as Lorenzo the Great, ruler of Florence, was part of Ficino's inner circle.

Ficino knew how the hymns had reappeared, but we do not. In 1423 Aurispa, an Italian historian, traveled to Constantinople in search of ancient Greek texts. He arrived in Venice with 238 treasures barely saved from the war between the Christians and the Turks. He brought back into the life of Europe the works of Plato, Sophocles, Aesychlus, and Plutarch. The Orphic hymns may have been in that collection, but we have no evidence that they were. Forty years later, Ficino translated the hymns into Latin. Ficino thought the hymns as we have them to be the verbatim record of the words of Orpheus himself, whose secret wisdom was taught to him by Hermes Trismegistus, his Egyptian equivalent. Then Orpheus passed this wisdom to Pythagoras, Ficino believed.

"I learned from Orpheus that love existed, and that it held the keys to the whole world, the whole power of magic consists in love. The work of magic is the attraction of one thing by another because of a certain affinity of nature," (Voss 2002) Ficino wrote, summing up Hermetic and magical theory in a sentence. For Ficino the hymns were not relics of a lost era, curiosities to be toyed with. He thought the words full of power. Or as Ficino himself wrote: "to the Egyptian priests medicine, music and the mysteries were one and the same study" (Voss 2007). But they were also magical rituals.

"Our spirit," Ficino wrote, "conforms to the rays of the heavenly spirit, which penetrates everything either secretly or obviously. It shows a far greater kinship when we have a strong desire for that life and are seeking a benefit that is consistent with it, and thus transfer our own spirit into its rays by means of love, particularly if we make use of song and light, and the perfume appropriate to the god, like the hymns that Orpheus consecrated to the cosmic deities" (Voss 2002).

By gathering up the right stones, plants, musical tones, colors, and incenses and performing the associated hymn on the right day, at the right time of day, in harmonious aspect to one's horoscope, Ficino believed purification and enlightenment could be achieved. He wasn't invoking the gods to appear before him and grant his wishes. He was tuning himself to their harmonics. He once wrote in a letter that, since he was born with Saturn conjunct the ascendant, he hoped to find a mate with a jovial disposition to balance him. But songs could do that, too. As in the days of Pythagoras, the right song could be used to convert fear, anger, or loneliness into contemplation of something holy.

Michael Allen has argued that the incenses accompanying the Orphic hymns were intended to provide smoke in which visible manifestations of the gods and goddesses could be encountered. The Parisian magus Éliphas Lévi described achieving just such a phenomenon when he magically invoked Apollonius of Tyana in London in 1854. Lévi wasn't certain what had responded to his ritual, but the figure he saw appeared in smoke from burning twigs and perfume he had chosen according to astrological and other correspondences that Ficino would have recognized.

"I have depicted the sublime, upward soaring of the heavenly mind," Ficino wrote. But in the world of Ficino and his friends, the hymns were not limited to ritual use. In his letters he writes about the pleasures of singing them alone or with good company. Such casual use still has the profound effect of tuning the souls of the performer and listeners.

In the writings of Iamblichus about Pythagoras, whom Ficino considered an Orphic initiate, Ficino found inspiration. Pythagoras, according to Iamblichus: "held that music contributes greatly to health, if used appropriately. The healing he got from music he called purification. In springtime a lyre player was seated in the center, and those who were good at singing sat round him in a circle and sang, to his accompaniment, songs of gratitude and praise, which raised their spirits and established inner harmony and rhythm. They also, at other times, used music as a kind of medicine. There were songs designed for afflictions of the soul, to counter despair and grief, and others to deal with rage or indignation. Those who were good at singing also happened to be mathematicians."*

Ficino never published his translations of the hymns from Greek to Latin. He circulated them only among friends, knowing that he was risking persecution by the church as a reviver of ancient superstitions. He became a skilled lyre player. His friends acknowledged that he played music of a quality that inspired the poet Naldi to say that Ficino was the reincarnation of Orpheus. Ficino's friend Poliziano wrote: "his wise lyre chases away grave thoughts and his voice follows the song springing up from under his expressive fingers, like Orpheus, interpreter of Apollo's songs. When he has finished, drawn on by the passion of the Muses I go home, to write verses, and, ecstatic I invoke Phoebus, I touch the divine lyre with my plectrum. His lyre is greater than the lyre of

*Translation by Ronnie Pontiac.

74

Thracian Orpheus, for he has brought back from the underworld what is, if I am not mistaken, the true Eurydice, that is Platonic wisdom with its all-embracing understanding" (Voss 2002).

In 1474 Poliziano's *Orfeo* was performed at carnival, with stage design by Leonardo da Vinci. The ultimate gift of creating music that can change your life and the lives of others cannot be gained by skill and wisdom only; the ultimate ingredient is what Ficino called "divine chance."

Among Ficino's friends was Count Pico della Mirandola, author of the famous "Oration on the Dignity of Man," where he wrote: "the human vocation is a mystical vocation that has to be realized in three stages: moral transformation, intellectual research and final perfection in identity with the absolute reality. This paradigm is universal, because it can be retraced in every tradition" (Copenhaver 2022).

The abandonment by Orpheus of Dionysus for Apollo was not accurate according to the founder of the reborn Platonic Academy, who wrote that Apollo is air and fire and Dionysus earth and water, for they are "inseparable companions." He and Pico joked that they were the Apollo and Dionysus of Florence.

In his *900 Theses,* Pico wrote: "The names of the gods that Orpheus sings are not names of deceiving demons, from whom evil and not good comes, but of natural and divine powers, distributed in the world by the true God for the great utility of man, if he knows how to use them" (Voss 2007).

To Ficino celestial movements were governed by the same laws as music, and musical intervals could be applied to astrological aspects. He compares the semi-sextile or thirty degree aspect to the second interval in music, a dissonant experience. But sixty degrees makes the harmonious sextile and the pleasing harmony of a musical third.

In his letter *The Orphic Comparison of the Sun to God,* Ficino explains: "It is certainly in the Sun that visible light is created from the intelligible light, and there also sight is created from understanding. For there understanding is no different from the light of consciousness, nor sight from visible light" (Voss 2002).

But was Ficino actually worshipping pagan gods? As Ficino scholar Angela Voss wrote: "He saw Orpheus, in his hymns, addressing the gods as multi-faceted, multi-layered cosmic principles, each one mirroring the diversity of creation yet all representing aspects of a single unified power—all the gods in each god and each in all" (2002).

Ficino counseled moderation and balance, writing: "When you fear Mars, set Venus opposite. When you fear Saturn, use Jupiter." This was a fellow who carried a flask of wine with him and encouraged wine drinking, but never to excess.

Nearing age sixty, Ficino looked back with pride on the Renaissance that flowered in his hometown of Florence. "This age, like a golden age, has brought back to light those liberal disciplines that were practically extinguished: grammar, poetry, oratory, painting, sculpture, architecture, music and the ancient singing of songs to the Orphic Lyre" (Voss 2002). But the mad monk Savanarola was just around the corner with his bonfires of the vanities that burned so many books, including the works of Ficino.

Almost a century after his death Ficino's work inspired the late sixteenth-century Académie de Poésie et de Musique (Academy of Poetry and Music) in France, founded by the poet Jean-Antoine de Baïf. There Protestant and Catholic musicians joined together to practice what they called Orphic singing, with the intention of creating a sympathetic magical harmony to stop the religious wars causing so much suffering in France.

The Occult Orpheus

About thirty years after Ficino died, German writer, soldier, lawyer, and physician Heinrich Cornelius Agrippa published his highly influential esoteric classic *Three Books of Occult Philosophy* (1533). In book one (*The Natural World*), chapter 71, he wrote: "When composing poems and speeches, to attract the power of any Star, or Deity, analyze the characteristics, how and what they influence, what processes they rule, and gather them into verses that praise, illustrate and celebrate their nature, while scorning what they work against." An example of this would be Saturn's traditional association with discipline, so in a ritual for Saturn it would be appropriate to condemn excess. Agrippa continues: "Know all their many names, and the names of those Intelligences that rule them. . . . If you desire more examples, research the hymns of Orpheus, with the right circumstances, which the wise understand, and with appropriate harmony, and complete attention, the most effective natural magic."

German physician, alchemist, and philosopher Paracelsus revolutionized medicine and the occult in the early 1500s. His own theory about human potential reflects the Orphic dichotomy of a child of earth and starry heaven: "The animal elements, instincts, and desires existed before the Divine Spirit illuminated them and made them into man. The animal soul of man is derived from the cosmic animal elements, and the animal kingdom is therefore the father of the animal man. If man is like his animal father, he resembles an animal; if he is like the Divine Spirit that may illuminate his animal elements, he is like a god. If his reason is absorbed by his animal instincts, it becomes animal reason; if it rises above his animal desires, it becomes angelic" (Hartmann 1896, 60).

Around 1605 Dr. Heinrich Khunrath published his *De Igne Magorum* in which he argued that the sun is the very fire of God. As an example of how someone can be illuminated by a ray of this divine power, he gave Orpheus. Khunrath was a Paracelsian physician and Hermetic philosopher with an enthusiasm for the kabbalah. He has been discussed as an initiatory link between John Dee and the Rosicrucians, but as always the proof, if it exists, is yet to be found. However, the influence of his books on Rosicrucian beliefs is obvious.

Orpheus went underground as Europe fought the long war between the Catholic Church and the Protestant nations. But we find him again as the Elizabethans begin their own cultural renaissance. "Orpheus with his lute" was the name of a popular Elizabethan song. Sir Francis Bacon in his *Of the Wisdom of the Ancients* (1609) wrote that Orpheus was the perfect symbol of philosophy. John Dee had Orpheus on his bookshelf, and he owed much of his own approach to ritual to Iamblichus.

Shakespeare offered his own succinct version of the myth, emphasizing the magic of music:

> *Orpheus with his lute made trees*
> *And the mountain tops that freeze*
> *Bow themselves when he did sing:*

To his music plants and flowers
Ever sprung; as sun and showers
There had made a lasting spring.
Every thing that heard him play,
Even the billows of the sea,
Hung their heads and then lay by.
In sweet music is such art,
Killing care and grief of heart
Fall asleep, or hearing, die.

In *Henry VIII* Shakespeare includes not a hymn of Orpheus but a hymn to Orpheus. He mentions Orpheus in three other plays: *Merchant of Venice, Rape of Lucrece,* and *Two Gentlemen of Verona.* At the wedding of Frederick V, elector Palatine, figurehead of the Protestant Union, and Princess Elizabeth, the daughter of King James, *Love's Labour's Lost* and many other plays were performed by Shakespeare's own company, the King's Men. The entertainment also included a ballet about Orpheus, criticized as "several hours too long." The loving but ill-fated marriage of Elizabeth and Frederick, and their ill-advised acceptance of the invitation to become king and queen of Bohemia, briefly provided a hothouse-like environment for the development of Rosicrucianism and European metaphysical religion. In one of the pageants, staged in the Palatinate for Elizabeth's delight, Orpheus rode a unicorn.

Manlius Severinus Boethius was born when the last emperor of the Western Roman Empire lost his throne to the barbarian general who instead of declaring himself emperor of Rome chose the title king of Italy. But the king of Italy lost his throne to the king of the Ostrogoths, Theodoric the Great, whom Boethius served faithfully as a Roman senator, consul, and judge.

In his masterpiece *The Consolation of Philosophy* (532 CE), Boethius presented chapters in verse he called songs. He included a song called "Orpheus and Eurydice." The plot points of his expression of the myth are similar to key points in *The Chymical Wedding of Christian Rosenkreuz*, published more than a thousand years later in 1616, possibly indicating a direct influence as Boethius was popular in Rosicrucian circles. Through a copper door in the floor of an ornate triangular tomb, Rosenkreutz entered an underground chamber where an eternal lamp flickered by a bed protected by curtains. When he peered through the curtains, Rosenkreuz saw Lady Venus naked on the bed, waiting to be resurrected. Perhaps he recalled the story of Actaeon turned into a stag and torn apart by his own hounds for daring to spy on Artemis as she bathed because, unlike Orpheus, Rosenkreutz did not look back.

In 1764 a book called *Orfei* was published. It collected together all known fragments of the Orphic tradition and included extensive notes from the translator, the scholar Johann Matthias Gesner. They were published three years after his death. Gesner was a schoolmaster, a rector, and a professor of poetry and eloquence at University of Göttingen, as well as the keeper of the university's library. He's better known today as the friend to whom Johann Sebastian Bach dedicated his Canon a 2 perpetuus BWV 1075.

Meanwhile, a rogue and libertine who had reinvented himself as the Baron de Hancarville made his name by brokering the sale of an extraordinary collection of antiquities to British antiquarian and diplomat Sir William Hamilton, resulting in the publication of a masterpiece of the engraver's art in four hand-painted volumes that are among the most beautiful ever published: *Collection of Etruscan, Greek, and Roman antiquities from the cabinet of the*

Honble. Wm. Hamilton, His Britannick Maiesty's envoy extraordinary at the Court of Naples (1767–1776). As the principal author, Hancarville used this opportunity to advance his theory of Orphism based on his study of vases he thought depicted the Eleusinian mysteries. According to Hancarville, this ancient wisdom of the unity of the divine was Phoenician and Etruscan but reached Greece through Orphic beliefs and practices. Like many students of the mysteries, Hancarville found proof of his theories everywhere. An egg next to a bull had to be Orphic even if it was made in Japan. Hancarville was also involved in the publication of three beautiful books of erotica. To his contemporaries, the engravings based on the art of antiquity were pornography. According to Hancarville, they were the artistic celebration of the joy of life and the beauty of nature.

In 1772 French philosopher Nicholas Boulanger's book *Antiquity Unveiled,* which had not been published during his lifetime, proposed that the mysteries of Orpheus enshrined beliefs similar to those of the Hindu Brahmans: a world that begins and ends only to begin again and so on infinitely, a world in which even the gods must be born and reborn in order to have existence. The survival of the soul, he argued, was a belief taught only to the elite until Christianity brought it to the common folk.

Antoine Court de Gébelin, in 1782, published his occult classic *Le Monde primitif, analysé et comparé avec le monde moderne* (The Primeval World, Analyzed and Compared to the Modern World). It was published as a series to subscribers that included Louis XVI, the king of France. Unfortunately for Louis, the wisdom in Gébelin's book did not help him avoid his date with the guillotine. In his book, Gébelin linked the twenty-two tarot trumps (including the fool card) with the twenty-two letters of the Hebrew alphabet for the first time in print. He believed that the sacred scribes of Egypt had translated the wisdom of their ancient Book of Thoth in the tarot.

Gébelin also included several of the Orphic hymns in his book. His eighteenth-century fanciful French translations from the ancient Greek texts have little resemblance to modern French or English translations. Here is our poetic rendition of his style in a verse from his *To Mousaios.*

> *I gave you instructions for predictions*
> *taken from bird flight, animal movements,*
> *and the guts of the sacrificed;*
> *I taught you how to decipher the dreams*
> *we are stricken with as we sleep at night;*
> *the interpretations of omens and wonders,*
> *and of the revolving stars;*
> *holy purification, source of happiness,*
> *with which we please the gods,*
> *and the rites to honor the dead!*

Since Orpheus did not condone animal sacrifice, the line about reading the omens of animal guts seems rather out of place, although this was a common custom among the ancient Greeks and Romans.

As we shall see, Orpheus has been transformed by centuries of popular culture. The wave of popularity that perhaps influenced American and English authors the most began with a rogue scholar by the name of Thomas Taylor, with the publication of his book *The Mystical Hymns of Orpheus* in 1792. His massive translations of the complete works of Plato and Aristotle and of Plotinus, Proclus, Porphyry, Maximus of Tyre, Iamblichus, and even more obscure philosophers were complex and difficult. They never made him any money. Writing his books bent his back and ruined his eyesight, but he was happy with the wife he had married when they were young and with their children, all chattering in Greek at the dinner table. His labors earned him the ridicule of most of his contemporaries. A critic writing in *Blackwood's Magazine* in 1825 dismissed him with: "he knows less than nothing of the language about which he is continually writing." However, the best Neoplatonic scholars today respect Taylor.

Mary Wollstonecraft, a founder of feminism, described her landlord Thomas Taylor's study as "the abode of peace." While he wrote, she would nap, with a feeling of safety she had never known before. William Blake was influenced by Taylor's work, and they knew each other. In vol. 44 issue 3 of *Blake: An Illustrated Quarterly* we can see Blake's annotations and underlined passages in his personal copy of Taylor's *The Mystical Initiations or, Hymns of Orpheus*. The next generation of English poets, Shelley and Byron, the rock stars of their era, also read Taylor. Other Taylor fans included Ralph Waldo Emerson, Bronson Alcott, and the mid-nineteenth-century transcendentalists; Thomas Johnson, Alexander Wilder, and the late-nineteenth-century American Platonists; many Theosophists, including Madame Blavatsky herself, who quoted him liberally; and the Golden Dawn of Samuel Liddell MacGregor Mathers, Wynn Westcott, and Aleister Crowley. As we have seen, Manly Hall's Philosophical Research Society reprinted the first edition in the late 1980s.

Taylor released the revised and enlarged second edition of *The Mystical Hymns of Orpheus* in 1824, the year Lord Byron died. Keats and Shelley were already dead. Blake was soon to follow. Still, it became one of the best-known books by Taylor because, apart from a translation of a hymn here or there in the work of Jane Harrison or Gilbert Murray, no other English translations were available for over a hundred years.

Three years later, in 1827, also in London, Julian Hibbert published his text of the hymns of Orpheus in the original Greek, which he called a typographical experiment because he printed the Greek without using the customary punctuation. A year later he published *Plutarchus and Theophrastus on Superstition*. In the preface he complained that none of the London booksellers wanted to carry *Orpheos Humnoi: The Book of the Orphic Hymns;* one dismissed it as "too thin." He adds that the literary magazines and newspapers ignored the numerous copies he sent out for review. Hibbert signs off: "I terminate this my Preface by consigning all 'Greek Scholars' to the special care of Beelzebub."

In the realm of the occult we find authors that might better be described as imaginative historians: historians who imagine patterns or definitions that fit a grand theory better than the facts. Some of them, such as Édouard Schuré, author of *The Great Initiates: A Study of the Secret History of Religions* (1889), and Godfrey Higgins, author of the learned but misguided *Anacalypsis* (1836), created mythology that was influential on later writers of what could be called alternate or secret histories.

Schuré was a student of Fabre d'Olivet, an eighteenth-century imaginative historian from France, writing around the same time as Thomas Taylor. In his *Hermeneutic Interpretation of the Origin of the Social State of Man,* d'Olivet created fanciful histories, claiming that he had unlocked the secret language of myth, including the angelic language underlying Hebrew. Orpheus received attention in d'Olivet's *The Golden Verses of Pythagoras*.

D'Olivet tells us that "the name of Orpheus, which signifies the Healer, the enlightened Physician, indicates a title given to this theocrat on account of the services that he rendered to his native country" (1995, 193). A theocrat believes in the union of church and state. So we are meant to draw the conclusion that

Orpheus was a powerful ruler. Indeed d'Olivet tells us that, at a time when faith in kings had declined and chaos loomed, Orpheus transferred the reins of power to the temples of the gods. D'Olivet also suggests that Orpheus was what we would call an avatar of the Hindu god Krishna.

D'Olivet worked in the French war ministry but admitted in his autobiography, published after his death, that instead of taking care of the business of the government he spent most of his time working on his books. He fell in love with a woman who died before they could marry. He claimed that she had appeared to him as an apparition several times after her death. She taught him the doctrine he taught others about the immortality of the soul. His Eurydice returned and explained the mysteries to him.

About a hundred years later Orpheus is a recurring theme in the works of Éliphas Lévi, the master occultist of nineteenth-century Paris. As Lévi wrote in *The Great Secret:* "The God of Hermes, of Pythagoras, of Orpheus, of Socrates, of Moses and of Jesus Christ was one and the same God and spoke to them all" (2000, 117).

Lévi was especially fascinated by the myth of the backward glance and by the violent death of Orpheus at the hands of the maenads. He used them as lessons about never falling too much in love, or he compared them to Christianity, where Jesus is not exactly torn apart but is tortured and killed by a mob. He considered Orpheus the first magus of ancient Greece. And he offered the interesting insight that Orpheus's invention of a music that made the stones and trees dance indicated that he understood relationships between numbers and the laws of harmony, which opened the way for a whole new world of practical inventions.

Almost another century later Robert Graves argued that the story of Orpheus was code for the oldest alphabet, an alphabet of trees and other seasonal and geographical references. Orpheus didn't literally make inanimate objects dance; he created a language out of familiar things, an alphabet that allowed new forms of self-expression. Setting the trees dancing would have been slang for using the tree alphabet masterfully. Graves thought the murder of Orpheus by women a vestige of the prehistoric sacred king sacrificed at the end of his reign. Graves was deeply influenced by Sir James George Frazer's enormous study *The Golden Bough,* which saw human sacrifice as the agricultural fertility ritual behind most ancient myths.

In 1882 Joséphin Péladan moved to Paris to become a writer for the influential illustrated arts weekly *L'Artiste*. Two years later he published *Le vice suprême* (The Supreme Vice). The popularity of the novel surprised many as it argued that the occult secrets of the sages of early Eastern civilizations could save humanity from itself. Péladan produced, wrote, and directed mystical plays that were performed through a series of six salons that he hosted called the Salon de la Rose + Croix. Among the plays performed was one called *Orpheus*. His orchestra played music by his friends Claude Debussy and Erik Satie, both of whom also played piano at the notorious Paris cabaret Le Chat Noir. The salon helped inspire the artists of the Symbolist movement and exhibited paintings by Gustave Moreau, including his masterpiece *Orpheus*.

Since Aleister Crowley claimed to be the reincarnation of Lévi, perhaps we should not be surprised that he was quite interested in Orpheus. The famous Abby of Thelema in Cefalu on the island of Sicily could, with its walls painted with powerful scenes, be said to resemble an Orphic mystery cave. Though Crowley never cites Jane Harrison or the other Cambridge Ritualists (a recognized group of classical scholars, so-called because of their shared interest in ritual), they are conspicuous perhaps by their absence. The

Thelemic hymn itself: "I am risen" has an Orphic theme.

Like his poetic idol Shelley, Crowley wrote a poem about Orpheus. Crowley divided the story of Orpheus into four parts. In the first, Orpheus tuned his lyre to the elemental forces. Then Orpheus lamented the death of Eurydice. Next he traveled to Hades. Finally, he sang on Mount Ida and fell to the maenads. Crowley meant it to be his greatest poem, the achievement that would guarantee his poetic fame, with dazzlingly complex rhyming schemes and ceremonial magical references enlightened by Buddhism, but the process of creating it was slow and troubling, and the result disappointed him. His friends were disappointed, too. Nevertheless, in 1905 Crowley released *Orpheus: A Lyrical Legend* in five two-volume editions, highly collectible thanks to their beautiful covers, each edition in a different color: olive, yellow, white, red, blue. There was also a one-volume edition on hemp paper.

Orpheus showed up in Crowley's periodical the *Equinox* in an article by Oliver Haddo: "There are certain Water Elementals whom Orpheus calls *Nereides*, dwelling in the more elevated exhalations of Water, such as appear in damp, cloudy Air, whose bodies are sometimes seen (as Zoroaster taught) by more acute eyes, especially in Persia and Africa" (1909).

Orpheus appeared in the next issue as a conqueror of hell in "The Poem of Hashish" by Charles Baudelaire and then incidentally in *Equinox,* vol. 1, no. 4, as a symbol of consummate musical skill. Absent from the following issue, he reappears in the sixth issue in the play *The Rite of Mars,* by Crowley, where Orpheus is asked to witness the victory of the "self-created Lord of Night." Later in the play, a poem by Shelley, "Hellas: Chorus" is quoted:

A loftier Argo cleaves the main,

Fraught with a later prize;
Another Orpheus sings again,
And loves, and weeps, and dies.

Absent from the next three issues, Orpheus returned in *Equinox,* vol. 1, no. 10, as Crowley translated Éliphas Lévi's *The Key of the Mysteries* (1959). Here Lévi tells the tale of the backward glance. In Lévi's version, Orpheus is a magus: "He wears the vestments of Grand Hierophant." Facing the east he sings of the history of creation, which is the history of love. Eurydice lies dead on the nearby bed. As he sings her cheeks redden. Crowley's translation does justice to Lévi's poetic pathos: "Unhappy one, do not look at her! Sing! Sing! Do not scare away the butterfly of Psyche, which is about to alight on this flower!"

10

More Popular Than Ever

Orpheus has never been so popular, and that's saying something considering how popular he was in ancient Rome. He's been a source of inspiration for artists, from the Renaissance to the present day and in all art forms: painting, sculpture, music, literature, film.

English painter John Macallan Swan's sensual painting *Orpheus* (1896) exemplifies the eroticism and the androgynous allure favored by artists of the late nineteenth century when representing Orpheus, including French sculptor Henri Peinte whose *Orphée endormant Cerbère* (1887) portrays Orpheus lulling to sleep the guard dog of Hades, three-headed Cerberus. The pose and physique are so similar it seems certain that Peinte inspired Swan.

The story of Orpheus was depicted in numerous works of art by masters spanning centuries, including the painters and sculptors Titian, Peter Paul Rubens, Giorgione, Auguste Rodin, Paul Klee, Picasso, Oskar Kokoschka, Max Beckmann, André Masson, and Isamu Noguchi.

The activist poet and art critic Guillaume Apollinaire first encountered the colorful abstractions of Robert Delaunay in 1912. The word he used to describe them became the name of an artistic movement: *Orphism.* In his book *The Cubist Painters: Aesthetic Meditations,* Apollinaire described Orphism as "the art of painting new totalities with elements that the artist does not take from visual reality, but creates entirely by himself. An Orphic painter's works should convey an untroubled aesthetic pleasure, but at the same time a meaningful structure and sublime significance" (as quoted in Warren 1988). According to Apollinaire, Orphism represented a move toward a completely new art form that would be to the fine arts what music is to literature. Robert Delaunay and his wife, Sonia, a Jewish French artist, were the driving force of this movement of strong colors and geometric shapes.

Orphic painters often referred to music in their titles; for example, Sonia Delaunay's *Kupka's Amorpha: Fugue in Two Colors* (1912). Her work included paintings, textile designs, and stage sets. She was the first living female artist to have a retrospective exhibition at the Louvre in 1964 and in 1975 was named an officer of the French Legion of Honor.

Orpheus the Tired Troubador painted in 1970 was one of the last works by Giorgio de Chirico, in some ways the father of Surrealism. De Chirico designed stage sets for mid-twentieth-century productions by Monteverdi and for Gluck's operas about Orpheus.

Astrid Zydower grew up in the disputed territory once Germany now Poland where she had childhood memories of being spit on for being a Jew. Her name literally means "born of a Jew." Her parents shipped her off to England just before they were sent to Auschwitz. She grew up to be a respected artist and a good friend of Charlie Watts, drummer of the Rolling Stones. Her works were commissioned by earls and Sir Mick Jagger. In 1984 she unveiled what could be considered her masterpiece, the nine-foot-tall bronze *Orpheus*. The eroticism of the late nineteenth-century artistic perspective remains: she leaves nothing to the imagination. This Orpheus, looking like a combination of Jim Morrison as the ultimate cat daddy and Christ on the cross, is boldly comfortable and confident in his masculinity.

Between 1600 and 2012, Orpheus has been the theme of

at least sixty-nine operas. Gluck, Monteverdi, Liszt, Offenbach, Telemann, Haydn, and, of course, Stravinsky who composed the ballet *Orpheus* are only a few on a long list of composers fascinated by the Orphic legend. Unfortunately, Claude Debussy's operatic work on the theme of Orpheus was never finished.

In 1993 Philip Glass debuted *Orphée,* a chamber opera, the first opera of his *Cocteau Trilogy.* In his version, Orpheus, a popular and successful poet married to Eurydice, herself a poet, finds himself held in contempt by the avant-garde. Losing his will to write, he becomes enamored of a princess whose angelic chauffeur is infatuated with Eurydice. The underworld Orpheus and Eurydice must visit is called the Zone. There Orpheus is interrogated. But true love prevails because the princess is willing to sacrifice herself so that Orpheus can be immortal. His married life resumes but with reborn creativity gained from this close encounter with death. Punished for her abuse of her power, the princess embraces oblivion. Perhaps the suggestion is that the renewed marriage of Orpheus and Eurydice will not be subject to death. What have they to fear, having already visited and returned from the Zone?

In Barre, Vermont, in 2006 a musical was born destined to win Tony awards and a Grammy. *Hadestown* debuted on Broadway in April 2019. It focuses on the relationships of not only Orpheus and Eurydice but also Hades and Persephone. The backward glance at the climax of the show drives home the tragedy. Just another example of how Orpheus continues to embody popular music.

Sinatra's teenage maenads, who flocked in crowds to his concerts and screamed as loud as any Beatles fans, the so-called bobby-soxers, were the first generation christened teenagers by advertising agencies. From 1944 until at least 1994 American maenads screamed for Orpheus, as portrayed by a sequence of young men who, according to sensible people, wore their hair too long and were somehow effeminate in their masculinity, what with their languid expressions, sultry voices, poetic lyrics, and suggestive dancing.

American Platonic scholar Jay Bregman recalls an experience, in a personal correspondence used by permission, that illustrates an Orphic moment he witnessed in mid-twentieth-century America. "I am a Be-Bopper," he writes, "who also digs Swing and I teach History of Jazz and play sax."

> So, it's March 17, 1956, I'm now a senior in high school—all the kids in the band got free tix to Dorsey Bros TV show. Dug the band—played Swing and modern Swing charts in high school. The first act comes on stage—this white cat who plays R&B like Blues-oriented stuff and sings—making—for the '50's risqué body movements. I hear piercing screaming behind me—teenage girls. Yeah, it's Elvis! After the show I look down a side street—53rd I think—he's surrounded now by the screaming teen maenads, an "Orphic" figure. I remember clearly one screaming: "I GOT HIS SCARF! I GOT HIS SCARF!"

In the late sixties and early seventies, MGM released records by an avant-garde rock group called Orpheus, whose sound was so influenced by the Doors it can only be described as the sincerest form of flattery. The twenty-first century has its own group named Orpheus, a popular Australian melodic death metal band. In 2004 Nick Cave and the Bad Seeds released their thirteenth record: *Abattoir Blues/The Lyre of Orpheus*.

In 2005 academic Geoffrey Sirc wrote an essay called "Composition's Eye/Orpheus's Gaze/Cobain's 'Journals,'" in which he references Orpheus and Kurt Cobain's journal writing, while contemplating the art of composition and how to best teach it to students. Critics dismissing the journals as juvenilia are compared to the maenads tearing Orpheus apart.

In 1945 while still attending Columbia University just after meeting Allen Ginsberg and William Burroughs, Jack Kerouac wrote his first novella. He never released it, but *Orpheus Emerged* was found after his death and published.

Randy Roark, who worked with Allen Ginsberg and William Burroughs for many years in personal correspondence used by permission, wrote about the influence of Orpheus on the beats:

Orpheus . . . one of my heroes! He made the trees and stones weep with his laments! When I was studying at Naropa my minor was in mythology and I had a conversation with Allen about it—he said that they weren't into myths except to the extent of mythologizing themselves. He said that (mostly via Burroughs' psychotherapeutic bent) they decided they wouldn't go down the route Pound and Joyce and even Tennessee Williams went—but they would instead approach their own lives as if they were mythic—look above, the mythic blue moon, or Moloch as the buildings of the financial district of S.F. etc.—and they were above trying to justify their writing via tying it to a classic myth—which they quite rightly claimed led to some of the most egregious poetry of the 40s and 50s. Jack Kerouac, he claimed, was a more useful 'myth' than the gods of ancient Greece. But—oddly enough in this case—he did say the one myth they all related to was Cocteau's filmic retelling of the story of Orpheus . . . especially in the scene where the poet is sitting in the car and getting his poetry from the radio. That scene—he said—became an image that was useful to the poet—that poetry did not come from the rational mind, but as if from a higher state of consciousness.

In his journal Roark recorded this comment by William Burroughs:

We no longer think that the sun is being driven around the planet by a Helios in a chariot—the world where the Gods made sense is over and by talking about myths we are trying to find meaning in something that has been emptied of meaning by time. Would you go back to Greek surgery, Greek science? Of course not. Plutarch killed off the gods once and for all when he reported how Tiberius, while sailing the Greek coast, heard a voice calling to him with the news that 'The Great Pan is dead!' But there are still people who haven't gotten the message.

Randy Roark gives another glimpse into the mind of Burroughs on the subject of ancient Greece.

One more: July 1983, at Allen's in the afternoon, Burroughs:
Hesiod in *Works and Days,* and the rest of his crew, were not writing mythology—they were writing Natural Science, history, and psychology. They were the Freuds of their time. But with some distance their science and history and psychology we see as metaphysics. The lesson for us is that if we could only see our own science, history and psychology from the point of view of an alien we would see it as metaphysics too. If we can do that, we can climb out of our own time's metaphysics and view it the same way we do the beliefs of the best and the brightest of 5th century B.C. Greece.

The Orpheus myth inspired the American playwright Tennessee Williams's 1957 drama *Orpheus Descending* with its snakeskin-jacketed, guitar-strumming male protagonist.

Jean Cocteau's *Orphic Trilogy,* three films spread over three decades—*The Blood of a Poet* (1930), *Orpheus* (1950), and

Testament of Orpheus (1960)—deconstructed the myth, giving it new life in a stream of dreamlike metaphors.

In 1959 the critically acclaimed film *Black Orpheus* came out. Made in Brazil by Marcel Camus, it was a retelling of the myth now set in Rio during Carnival.

The filmmaker D. A. Pennebaker filmed Bob Dylan's 1965 tour at the height of Dylan's iconic status. The documentary he released in 1967 he gave the Orphic title *Don't Look Back.*

Literary critic Harold Bloom published his classic *The American Religion* in 1992. There he described spirituality in the United States as American Orphism. He christened the New Age movement California Orphism. The same year the Orpheus myth inspired a horror comedy film called *Highway to Hell,* about a couple that elopes to Vegas. The groom gives chase when the bride gets arrested by a hell cop and is dragged to hell to wed Satan. Real Hell's Angels bikers and golden-haired cannibals are among the challenges he faces. It's a cult classic, with cameos by Ben and Jerry Stiller and Gilbert Gottfried as Hitler.

In 2000 a two-hour docudrama *Orpheus and Eurydice* was released, narrated by Oliver Reed, by the production company best known for their *Treasures of Ancient Hellas* video series. Reminiscent at times of the first *Star Trek* TV series, with hints of *Monty Python and the Holy Grail,* liberties are taken for the sake of melodrama.

But 2000 also saw a sublime musical ritual in an ancient church in London involving Shakespearean actor and theater director Mark Rylance, vocalists of high attainment, and musician and Ficino scholar Angela Voss. The Marini Consort's performance *Secrets of the Heavens* included recitals of Thomas Taylor translations of hymns followed by singers singing them in the original Greek, with the incense specified for each.

In 2016, on YouTube, Bulgarian filmmaker Stiliyan Ivanov released his documentary *Orpheus,* an appropriately theatrical, visually beautiful survey of history and mythology, where viewers can see artifacts discussed in this book.

Orpheus has also been a popular theme in comic books, from Neil Gaiman's *The Sandman* to the first African American superhero, Gotham City's comic book character Orpheus. His story was entwined with Batman, first appearing in *Batman: Orpheus Rising* in 2001. This short-lived comic book series ended in 2002, when the villain Black Mask killed Orpheus.

In 1996 the TV show and comic book series *Xena Warrior Princess* featured Orpheus as a recurring character. This Orpheus loved fame and glory too much so Eurydice left him for Hercules. But then Bacchus killed her. Orpheus used his music to hold back the Bacchae. He brings Eurydice back to life, but she dies again at the hands of Bacchus. Finally, with Xena's help, Orpheus slays Bacchus.

In New Orleans for Mardi Gras in 1993, the Krewe of Orpheus was founded by, among others, Harry Connick and his son Harry Connick Jr. A *krewe* is an organization or association that stages a parade. Since its inception, the Krewe of Orpheus has selected a celebrity monarch to reign over its parade. Celebrity monarchs have included film director Quentin Tarantino, Bret Michaels of the glam metal band Poison, vampire story author Anne Rice, and music legend Stevie Wonder.

In 2003, White Wolf Publishing released a game called *Orpheus,* which included six rulebooks, among them one called *Shades of Gray.* A 2009 freeware game called *Don't Look Back* is a modern interpretation of the myth.

In 2023 connoisseurs enjoy the handcrafted delights of beers called Transmigration of Souls and Life.Death.Life.Truth, thanks to the Orpheus Brewing Co. in Atlanta, Georgia.

The Backward Glance

Speaking to the dead in ancient Greece was not unique to Orpheus. It happened in the *Iliad,* when the recently killed Patroclus appeared to Achilles in a dream. How can Achilles sleep, he wonders, while his best friend's body waits for the pyre and his soul is held outside the land of the dead? Patroclus predicts that Achilles, too, will die under the walls of Troy.

In the *Odyssey* communication between the dead and the living was messy. Odysseus visited the land of the dead where he dug a pit. He poured libations for the dead. After many prayers, he killed the animals he brought to sacrifice, filling the pit with their blood. The ghosts of the dead swarmed, so many Odysseus couldn't name them all. He came to speak to his mother and to the prophet Tiresias, but he also spoke with Achilles and with the great king Agamemnon, who told him how he made it home only to be caught in a net in his bath and murdered by his own wife and her lover.

In his elegant book *In the Dark Places of Wisdom,* Peter Kingsley reminds us that a famous poem about Orpheus written by a Pythagorean claims that the journey of Orpheus was a dream incubated near a volcano at a site sacred to dream oracles. In the poem the oracular powers of Apollo are shared by the goddess Nyx. Later, Greeks such as Plutarch insisted that the god of light and reason could have nothing to do with the goddess of primal darkness. But modern research indicates that Apollo did have a dark side, a night side. After all, the wolf was his sacred animal.

A fragment by a little known writer from four hundred years before the birth of Jesus was the first to give the wife of Orpheus a name, Eurydice, literally "Wide Justice." A strange name for the wife of Orpheus, more appropriate for Persephone, queen of the dead, who shared her husband's power to judge souls. Could a secret lurk behind that name? Perhaps that Orpheus learned the divine secrets not from Apollo but Persephone?

The separation of Orpheus and Eurydice just after their wedding happened because a shepherd overcome by her beauty tried to kill Orpheus and take her by force. Orpheus and Eurydice ran, hand in hand, through the woods, until her hand slipped out of his. Then he discovered her dead from a snake bite. Who was this man? His name was given as Aristaeus, but this creates a contradiction since Aristaeus is an ancient Greek god of beehives, grape vineyards, and olive orchards, a protector of shepherds. As a son of Apollo he could be called the half brother of Orpheus. His name means "Most Excellent."

Virgil tells us, or perhaps invented the story, that Aristaeus lost his bees because of what he had done to Orpheus and Eurydice. We don't know if this was a spontaneous protest, or if the songs of Orpheus inspired the bees to rebel. A strange detail adds an ironic note to the story of Aristaeus, that his son was the hunter Actaeon who was turned into a stag and torn apart by his own hounds. Like Orpheus, Aristaeus was torn into pieces, like the baby Dionysus when the Titans murdered him.

Virgil and Ovid gave us the melodramatic focus on the

backward glance that has charmed so many. In book eleven of Ovid's *Metamorphoses,* Apollo saves Orpheus's head from a snake attack in Lesbos, while Dionysus punishes the maenads for killing Orpheus. In the second century CE, the astrologer Ptolemy reported that Orpheus and Eurydice became the constellation Lyra, to shine forever as a symbol of love.

But the earliest Roman depictions of Orpheus showed him bringing Eurydice back into the sunlight. Early Christians knew Orpheus as a savior, not a failure. Like Jesus, Orpheus returned from death. His trip to the underworld to save Eurydice was similar to Jesus saving souls from hell. During the Middle Ages scholars thought Orpheus fit Christianity rather nicely. As we have seen, Orphic ideas influenced Dante's *The Divine Comedy.* From there, the backward glance reached the world of opera.

What is the meaning of the backward glance and the loss of Eurydice? Why does it haunt us so? Is it merely a *memento mori,* a reminder of the finality of mortality? In the Middle Ages, it was a symbol of human weakness, illustrating the way even the most dedicated among us, the holiest, cannot escape those moments of desire for material pleasures. The artist unable to grasp beauty, the desperate desire of the lover for the beloved, the overeagerness of passion, betrayal by insecurity, the evasiveness of memory—the backward glance has been a mirror for generations, not escaping the scrutiny of Freudians and Jungians. The latter finally reversed it, making it a symbol of individuation and the achievement of autonomy.

Esoteric psychologist Carl Jung wrote that the Orphic mysteries "kept alive the old Dionysiac religion rooted in the art of agriculture" (1968, 135). He recorded details about Orphism, such as his observation that a ram is the symbol of the sunrise in the Orpheus frescoes in the cemetery of Domitilla. Jung used the Orphic myth of Dionysus torn apart by the Titans, and the death of Orpheus at the hands of the maenads, as lessons about the limits of creativity and imagination: one may experience the magical quality of creating the right thing in the right place at the right time for the right reasons, but such perfection can't be sustained.

The idea that Orpheus deliberately looked back, as a symbol of renunciation, goes back at least as far as John of Garland in 1234 CE. But the backward glance is not exclusively Orphic or European. As A. H Gayton wrote: "Tales of the recovery of a beloved person from the land of the dead are common in North American mythology" (1935).

In personal correspondence used by his permission, Randy Roark writes:

There's a whole genre of Native American myth called "Orphic Myths." This one from the Nez Perce (Montana to Washington) came from a book called *Reading the Fire.* He said it's one of the most detailed, but they're all more or less the same and are one of the few stories that involve a vision of a "happy hunting ground" after death where all your friends are and everything's cool.

Coyote's wife died and he was inconsolable. He was so sad that he did none of his work, and the Earth suffered, and this drew the attention of the Death Spirit. He came down and said to Coyote, you can have your wife back, but you must follow me and do everything I do and do everything I tell you to do. So, they head off to the Land of Death and it's dark and foggy. The DS says at one point, "Look at the horses" and Coyote can't see anything but says, "Yes, I see them." Later, DS says, "Let's eat some berries" and Coyote pretends to eat berries. Bunch of that and then they come to a teepee with no door. But the DS reaches out and opens the invisible tent flap. Coyote's told to sit down. He can see nothing. He sits. He hears a lot of whispering around him, and he's told he's surrounded by the dead, who are surprised to see him there. He is told his wife is sitting next to him and has brought him food. He sees nothing and pretends to eat the food. In the morning, the DS says he can walk back to Earth and his wife will follow him. He cannot touch her or talk to her until they get back. They walk and every day she's a little more visible. One morning she is as real as she was before death, and he was moved to hug her and she screamed "Don't touch me" but it's too late and she disappears.

A visit to the underworld with an ill-fated backward glance is found in Japanese mythology. In *The Masks of God: Oriental Mythology,* Joseph Campbell shares a story from *Kojiki* (古事記), which means "Records of Ancient Matters" (1962, 467).

His Augustness the Male Who Invites and his younger sister Her Augustness the Female Who Invites do what creator gods do and from their union are born the islands of Japan along with the sacred powers—the holy spirits of earth, ocean, seasons, winds, mountains, forests, moors, and fire. Fast Burning Fire scorches his mother when he is born. As she sickens, more sacred powers are born from her bodily fluids. But then to save the world she helped create, Her Augustness the Female Who Invites removes herself from the heaven she shared with her brother and their children.

In grief His Augustness the Male Who Invites takes up his sword and beheads his child Fast Burning Fire, from whose body parts, and from the blood dripping from different parts of his sword, more spirits are born.

Like Orpheus, the grief-stricken His Augustness the Male Who Invites decides to visit the underworld and bring back his beloved sister so that together they can finish the work of creation. She comes out to meet him.

She wants to return, but like Persephone in Hades, she has eaten of the food of the realm of the dead, so she cannot leave. She asks him to wait while she consults with the sacred powers of the place. Like Orpheus, who was not allowed to look back, His Augustness the Male Who Invites is told he must not search for his sister in the darkness of the underworld.

Growing impatient at her long absence, His Augustness the Male Who Invites breaks off a tooth from the the comb he wears on the left side of his hair. He sets it afire, making it a torch. He finds his beloved, but her body, full of maggots and spirits of thunder, horrifies him. Angry because his disobedience has brought her shame, she sends one avenging sacred power after another to attack her brother. Finally, she comes after him herself. To stop her, he picks up a huge rock and blocks the Level Pass of the Land of Night. Her Augustness the Female Who Invites then becomes the Great Spirit of the Land of Night. Every day she kills a thousand of her brother's people, but every day he causes fifteen hundred women to give birth.

Here we have a story of a brokenhearted lover visiting the underworld to win back his beloved, the stipulation that he not look at her until she returns, and a terrible price paid for being impatient.

The earliest telling of the story of Savitri and Satyavan is found in the *Vana Parva* (Book of the Forest) of the *Mahabharata*. For many years the king of Madra lived like a monk, offering flowers and other sacred gifts to the sun god. He did this because his wife bore him no children. At last, the sun god was moved to grant the king's wish. He would have a daughter. Savitri was so beautiful, so pure, and so intelligent that no man dared to ask for her hand in marriage. Her father gave up trying to arrange a wedding, so

Savitri searched for the man who would be her husband.

Savitri found Satyavan, a woodcutter who was once a prince but whose father had lost not only his kingdom but his sight. Satyavan will live only one year after they marry, Narada warns Savitri. Narada, an avatar in the form of a wandering musician sage, is somewhat like Orpheus but without the tragic love story and violent ending.

The marriage of Savitri and Satyavan is happy. They live a simple life in the forest with his mother and father, but then the appointed day arrives. Refusing to leave his side, Savitri goes with Satyavan to work.

At first, all is well but then Satyavan complains that he feels exhausted. He lies on the ground with his head on Savitri's lap while she soothes him. After his last breath, the creatures of Yama, the god of death, arrive to claim his soul. But the shining holiness of Savitri blinds them. They return to Yama empty-handed, a rare event. Yama personally goes to retrieve Satyavan's soul. He is immune to Savitri's purity.

As Yama departs with Satyavan's soul, Savitri quietly follows. Yama, sensing her presence, glances back and sees her. He tells her to go home. She argues that she is only doing what is right: a dutiful wife should never leave her husband. Yama is impressed by her devotion. He offers to grant any wish, except her husband's life, of course. She wishes for her father-in-law to be able to see again. Yama grants her wish and kindly tells her to return home. Then he continues on his way.

Yama glances back only to see Savitri still following him. He orders her to go home. How can it be right for her to go home alone on an unknown path, she responds. Impressed by her clever argument, he grants her another wish, any wish but her husband's life. With the second wish she restores her father-in-law's kingdom. Yama assures her that now she will safely find her way home.

She must not insult his generosity any further by disobeying him again. He sets off.

Yama glances back and there is Savitri a few steps behind him. He scowls as he commands her to turn back. She praises him as the one who brings justice. Is it not her duty to attend to such an illustrious being? Charmed again, Yama grants her a third wish, with the prior stipulation. Savitri wishes to bear a hundred sons. Without thinking it through, Yama grants her wish. Then Savitri reminds him that a pure wife will be faithful to her husband after his death, therefore for her wish to be granted, Satyavan must be returned to the living. Yama realizes he has been defeated. He blesses them both with long lives. Satyavan wakes up in her lap as if from a dream. Yama seems to be a better sport than Hades.

What of ancient Egypt? We have Osiris torn into pieces, his brokenhearted wife, Isis, chanting magical spells as she travels searching for him, in the hope of resurrecting him. Isis, however, resurrects Osiris in a way quite different from what Orpheus attempted.

The idea of a journey into the land of the dead to retrieve a loved one must have been especially relatable during the era when raids by enemies separated families. Negotiating or fighting for the release of hostages could have became a metaphor about bargaining with death.

But journeys to other worlds, especially to the abode of the dead are a common practice of shamanism, and Thrace, where most Greeks believed Orpheus came from, was a territory where shamans flourished for centuries. Although in 2016 Jan Bremmer wrote in "Shamanism in Classical Scholarship: Where Are We Now?" that the "shamanic paradigm" had been "dismantled," some scholars continue to argue that Orpheus represents an attempt to rationalize the beliefs and powers of the shaman, who used songs as magical tools, who visited other worlds, and who knew the sacred names.

The Evolution of Eurydice

In some of the earliest tellings of the myth of Orpheus, his wife is not called Eurydice but Agriope, the Wild-Eyed, and there are versions where she saved him from Hades. As we have seen, the perception of Orpheus has not remained static over the centuries. He became a troubadour and a brave knight, has been compared to both Jesus Christ and King David, and was said to have been a student of Moses.

The backward glance has inspired an evolution of not only Orpheus but even more so of Eurydice. For example, the world of opera changed forever when Gluck decided that the story of the backward glance needed a feel-good ending. The unexpected successful rescue of Eurydice by Orpheus, after so many tragic operas about their lost love, was a triumphant success that changed the course of future operas.

As we shall see, more recently among female artists, Eurydice has evolved considerably and delightfully. Orpheus has become a self-obsessed boyfriend. Eurydice doesn't want to be his muse or the subject of his poems. She doesn't want to serve his fame or his religion, and in one poem, by Carol Ann Duffy, Orpheus is transformed into a sulking stalker Eurydice can't forget quickly enough.

We begin with Eurydice the mystery. In the early sources she had no name, no description, no voice. On the one hand, this emphasizes the way death has made her entirely unavailable to Orpheus and to us. Humanities professor Helen Sword calls her a "mythological nobody" (1989, 408).

The alienation of Eurydice, her reduction to a mere image, foreshadows modern media where the image on the screen may dominate and drive the lives of people who watch it, the way memory and mourning drove Orpheus. In the same way, the disembodied head of Orpheus foreshadows radio and audio recordings that allow the voice to continue when the body is absent. Pythagoras teaching from behind a veil is another example of a disembodied voice.

No one addressed this absence of Eurydice with more depth and eloquence than twentieth-century literary scholar Maurice Blanchot in works like his collection of essays *The Gaze of Orpheus*. For Blanchot, Eurydice is "the profoundly obscure point toward which art and desire, death and night, seem to tend" (Gill 1996, 157). For Blanchot, the backward glance is a symbol of the way art and literature are an ever-vanishing horizon. "Orpheus's mistake," writes Blanchot, "may be the desire to see and possess Eurydice, though his destiny is to only sing about her. He is only Orpheus when he sings, the only relationship he could have with Eurydice is in songs" (1981, 43).

From this perspective, Orpheus shares with Aristaeus, the author of his misery, the fault of having tried to possess Eurydice. Ultimately, Eurydice must be content with having been loved and Orpheus with having his heart broken to ripen his destiny as a teacher of sacred secrets. As the French poet Mallarmé put it: "he became who he was meant to be."

The German poet Rilke demonstrated his belief that art is more important than love in his own life. He separated from his wife six months after the birth of their first child because fatherhood interfered with his writing.

During the winter of 1922 in the Alps, Rilke felt the overwhelming presence of the source of all poetry, and when he searched for a name for this shining being he found Orpheus. Orpheus had already been haunting him with inspiration through poems, found postcards, and works of art. Under this undeniable influence, Rilke was compelled to write down fifty-five sonnets, his masterpiece *The Sonnets to Orpheus*. The sonnets are dedicated to Wera Ouckama Knoop, the daughter of a Dutch novelist who was a friend of Rilke's. Rilke's daughter had been a close friend of Wera's, but Rilke had met her only a few times.

Wera was a beautiful child with a bright future in ballet until she became very sick. No longer able to dance, she learned how to be a musician. As her health failed, her creative drive was reduced to drawing. She died not long after reaching age nineteen. Two years after her death, after an exchange of sentimental letters with Rilke, her mother sent him Wera's sixteen-page handwritten record of her anguished months of dying, which he read on the night of January 1, 1922.

On February 2, 1922, Rilke claimed he was possessed by Orpheus and wrote the sonnets. Wera was, at least as a muse, the Eurydice to Rilke's Orpheus.

In his poem "Orpheus. Eurydice. Hermes," Rilke painted a picture of an impatient Orpheus, concerned with his own agenda, reactions, and reflections. In Rilke's poetry, Orpheus does not escape the fate of Eurydice. His name and teachings may live on, but the one he loves forgets him.

> *And when, abruptly,*
> *the god reached out his hand to stop her, saying,*
> *with sorrow in his voice: He has turned around—,*
> *She could not understand. She softly answered Who?*

◆

In the distance, dark before the bright exit,
someone stood, whose face
was unrecognizable. (Balfiore 2007)

By giving us Eurydice's point of view, Rilke gives Orpheus the helpless anonymity that was once only hers. How different this is from Virgil's melodramatic Eurydice who scolded Orpheus, asking rhetorically what madness made him look back and ruin both their lives? In this image of Orpheus's effacement, Rilke captures the alienation of modern life and the dehumanization occurring in societies all over the world, during the pause between two world wars.

In 1925 American poet Hilda Doolittle, better known as H.D., wrote a poem called "Eurydice" about the breakup of her marriage. Her Orpheus is a narcissist: "what was it you saw in my face? / the light of your own face, / the fire of your own presence?" He is so vain, and ambitious, he dares turn Hades itself into a stage for the demonstration of his genius. He does not love her. He loves the image of himself loving her.

In the United States it wasn't until the 1960s that women were allowed to open bank accounts. As gender roles have evolved and women are gaining the right to choose how they will contribute to society, so too Eurydice has evolved. Now she has the emotions and perspectives long denied her. For her the backward glance has become not a second death but an affirmation of independence and the right to have her own way of being. If her fate was to serve the mission of Orpheus, then let his memory of her perform that task. The soul of Eurydice lives in another world where she is herself and happier.

Contemporary female poets—including Margaret Atwood, Scottish UK Poet Laureate Carol Ann Duffy, Pulitzer Prize-winning poet Jorie Graham, Laurie Sheck, Jody Gladding, Irish poet Eavan Boland, and Louise Glück, the twelfth US Poet Laureate, to mention only a few—have responded to Eurydice's plight by giving her a voice to express resentment, frustration, and even love for Orpheus as her selfish husband, exposing his poetic ego and his dependence on her death. He turns because he cannot trust her. He cannot resist his need to manage her.

Louise Glück's Orpheus worries: "Who knows what you'll tell the furies / when you see them again." But he's confident in his fame: "I sang to them; they will remember me."

In Adrienne Rich's poem "I Dream I'm the Death of Orpheus," Eurydice is a maenad driving a black Rolls-Royce, with her dead poet in it, "through a landscape of twilight and thorns . . . a woman sworn to lucidity, who sees through the mayhem, the smoky fires of these underground streets."

Margaret Atwood's Eurydice in her poem of the same name is happier away from Orpheus. She says about Eurydice: "You would rather have gone on feeling nothing, emptiness and silence; the stagnant peace of the deepest sea, which is easier than the noise and flesh of the surface."

Carol Ann Duffy's Eurydice is glad to be rid of the annoying narcissist she married and is dismayed that even in Hades she isn't safe from him: "Ye Gods / a familiar knock knock at Death's door / Him. / Big O. / Larger than life. / With his lyre / and a poem to pitch, with me as the prize."

Poet Gregory Orr has also reimagined Eurydice: "When I put on flesh again it felt like a soiled dress." She longs to return to the freedom of having no body. The idea of resuming her relationship with Orpheus makes her feel claustrophobic.

At the eve of the twenty-first century, Israeli artist and psycho-analyst Bracha Ettinger created her haunting Eurydice series. Collages and halted photocopies of family photographs, aerial surveillance photos from World War II, and newspaper articles about the Holocaust, are mixed with residual ink, and slowly oil painted abstraction and textures, to convey the disassociation and other nuances of transgenerational transmission of epigenetic trauma.

In 2004 Polish American poet Czeslaw Milosz published a poem in the *New Yorker* titled "Orpheus and Eurydice" about the death of his second wife, historian Carol Thigpen. In this poem, the backward glance becomes a comment on the shadow mortality casts over love: "It happened as he expected. He turned his head and behind him on the path was no one."

In 2021 American playwright Sara Ruhl published *Eurydice*. In Hades Eurydice sees her father again. But remembering Orpheus and the world she left behind is a struggle, a challenge she may not be able to meet.

The most common opinions about Eurydice, of male scholars, are an uncomfortable indictment. Is Eurydice, in the early versions of her myth, without emotions because a manly storyteller in those days would never stoop to consider the perspective of a mere woman? She is helpless as Orpheus and Hades decide her fate. Later we are asked to imagine Eurydice as a silenced victim, a forgetful shade sacrificed to the glory of Orpheus. When finally given a voice by Virgil, she reprimanded Orpheus like an estranged wife. Then we are asked to believe that she gladly sacrificed herself so that her husband could achieve his potential.

Could Orpheus and Eurydice represent the soul and the body, never quite wed? Eurydice the body dies, but Orpheus the soul continues singing, even after the disassembling of his body. As always, Eurydice remains an enigma, mysteriously obscure under the projections of centuries, refusing to be known, like a mirror mistaken for what it reflects.

13

The Mystical Purpose

The songs of Orpheus and the gold leaves are theater in miniature. They can be read as fairly straightforward requests for health, wealth, peace, and the other joys of life, for freedom from fear and anger, and for abundant harvests. But there is more to it than that. In the ancient Near East, rites to heal the sick sought to restore the harmony of the cosmos by bringing the patient back into harmony. The hymns by addressing all the powers of nature and the divine allow us to restore each facet of our forgotten understanding of the cosmos.

Her scholarship is dated now, and many of her conclusions suspect, but Jane Harrison had a deep knowledge of her subject. In her *Prolegomena to Greek Religion* she wrote: "The religion of Orpheus is religious in the sense that it is the worship of the real mysteries of life, of potencies (δαίμωνς) [daimons] rather than personal gods [Θεοί Theoi]; it is the worship of life itself in its supreme mysteries of ecstasy and love. . . . It is these real gods, this life itself, that the Greeks, like most men, were inwardly afraid to recognize and face, afraid even to worship. Now and again a philosopher or a poet, in the very spirit of Orpheus, proclaims these true gods, and asks in wonder why to

111

their shrines is brought no sacrifice" (Harrison 1903, 657). Porphyry wrote in *On Abstinence:*

> Worship the highest in pure and profound silence, with pure thoughts glorified by the divine. Having connected and conformed ourselves to the sacred, we should approach the sublime with reverence that reflects appreciation on the sacred and protection on us. Only a soul liberated from worldly attachments, an intelligent eye of conscious light, can contemplate the highest. But to the supreme deity's children we can present songs composed intelligently. Everywhere tradition offers the first harvest of the gifts received from the divine. As farmers offer handfuls of fruit and grain, so can we offer purest thoughts, the soul's excellence, thanking the gods for the inspiration they give us, and for planting seeds in our minds, ideas about divine qualities, about how they communicate with us, revealing themselves to our mental sight, to shine sacred splendors on us, to save us.*

Thomas Taylor wrote in "A Dissertation on the Life and Theology of Orpheus":

> If it should be asked, in what the power of prayer consists, according to these philosophers? I answer, in a certain sympathy and similitude of natures to each other; just as in an extended cord, where when the lowest part is moved, the highest presently after gives a responsive motion. Or as in the strings of a musical instrument tempered to the same harmony; one chord trembling from the pulsation of another, as if it were endued with sensation from symphony.

---

*Translation by Ronnie Pontiac.

So in the universe, there is one harmony though composed from contraries; since they are at the same time similar and allied to each other. For from the soul of the world, like an immortal self-moving lyre, life everywhere resounds, but in some things more inferior and remote from perfection than in others—we must not conceive, that our prayers . . . draw down divine beneficence; but that they are rather the means of elevating the soul to these divinities . . . for the divine irradiation, which takes place in prayer, shines and energizes spontaneously, restoring unity to the soul, and causing our energy to become one with divine energy—as the great Theodorus says, "all things pray except the first." (Taylor 1981, 71)

In the Orphic hymn *Mise,* for example, consider the multiple meanings of:

> Notice our holy rites,
> reward reverence
> with seasons ideal
> for the growth of good fruit.

The request is not only for the right amounts of heat, cold, sunshine, and rain to produce an abundant harvest but also for a long life with appropriate successes for its various stages, because the fruit to be ripened is the soul. Through the power of the hymns, words become a means of invoking divine essence not only in self but in the world.

A Note on Incense

In the original text, as we have it, not every hymn included incense. In some cases, as with Hades and Persephone, it may be that the last thing the mystic desired was to provide smoke for a feared deity of the dead to manifest through. Most of the incenses provided by the text are either frankincense, storax, myrrh, or aromatic herbs. The mystics would have imported their storax from Phoenicia and their frankincense and myrrh from Arabia.

The word *storax* comes from the late Latin *styrax*. The *styraka* of the hymns is not the same as the storax in stores today, the gum of *Liquidambar styraciflua*. Styrax benzoin comes closest to the storax of ancient times. A careful searcher can find boutique occult supply businesses offering the original thing in handcrafted small batches.

The subtlety of botanical correspondences enriches understanding of the use of incense or herbs as sacrifices, or wine and oil as poured libations. For example, Persephone's crown was woven of asphodel flowers, the flower, according to Homer's *Odyssey,* that filled the meadows where the dead forget. Often planted on tombs, it became known as the food of the dead.

Asphodel had its medicinal uses in those days. The ancient

Persians used it to make a well-known strong glue. Asphodel bulbs, heated in fire, explode like fireworks when knocked against a rock. Was this considered evidence of spiritual power? In the asphodel fields the dead were thought to be unable to focus; they simply drifted, without blood, like smoke that never dissipates. Having lost all sense of self, or power to act or communicate, they were stuck in the mire of having wasted their unexamined lives, without heroic or virtuous accomplishments.

We may not be able to exactly replicate ancient incenses, but we can find more readily available choices that reflect some of the same depth of correspondence.

A Note on the Translation

The hymns can inspire a sense of monotheism despite being a sacred scripture of polytheism. Basic similarities give the impression that the same deity is being viewed by different cultures, or according to different facets of understanding, not unlike the ninety-nine names of God in Islam. "Of many names" is a common phrase in the original hymns, which mention places in Greece, the Near East, and Egypt.

However formulaic and haphazard the hymns seem, the great beauty and true poetry in many of the lines may point to an original that has been lost through so many translations and transliterations. The hymns have been divided and compiled by so many hands, that only fragments remain, embedded in the dross of the centuries.

In 2013 a new definitive translation of the Orphic hymns by Apostolos Athanassakis and Benjamin Wolkow was published. Their book, *The Orphic Hymns,* is a significant step forward for English readers, revealing the stark splendor while sparing us the formulaic repetitions.

In the renditions that follow, the formulas have been minimized to make the language as immediate as possible. Where hymns seemed especially devoid of the character of the deities addressed, liberties are taken. Details drawn from myth and cult practice enhance the experience for those who have no associations for these obscure names of all but forgotten deities. Those who used these hymns would have known such details.

Literary faults may have spiritual virtues. Repetition, for example, inspires trance. The abbreviated diction of the hymns—at times they become little more than a list of attributes—is itself an important ancient form of worship, of attaining a deity's attention, and takes on another dimension when subtle aspects of context and metaphorical overtones become known.

For example, in the sacred song "Earth," heedless of the fate of Onomacritus, we've taken the liberty of mistranslating a word. "Seed of the eternal universe" should be "seat of the eternal universe." But the English word *seat* lacks certain overtones of meaning associated with the same word in ancient Greek. Proclus wrote: "heaven must be imagined as remaining entire in its own seat—this 'seat' of heaven is the place of the body," or as Michael Griffin explained in his article "Proclus on Place as the Luminous Vehicle of the Soul": "light 'embraces the body as its seat of motion and movement" (2012).

Just as the teeming organization of the body filled with microscopic births and deaths, second by second, is the focal point and fixed state of a soul, so Earth is considered the focal point and fixed state of the entire cosmos, of the ultimate harmony of the universe.

We have recklessly added stanzas and added new hymns, one to replace a missing hymn called "Number." Asteria appears twice, in our version of the hymn to Leto and also in her own hymn, which we wrote. In other words, this is a poetic work, not a scholarly translation, having been created with the intent of providing a text for enjoyment as literature, play, and ritual.

The sacred songs of Orpheus exist in that moment when reverential and even fearful attempts by worshippers to draw the attention of the deity by praising divine attributes shifted to compelling spirits, angels, or devils to do the bidding of the magus who knows their secret names.

The songs and myths of Orpheus arose from the nexus of history, drama, myth, music, philosophy, symbology, cosmology, literature, art, and performance to influence and perhaps define Western culture, and especially counterculture, for over two thousand years.

The Orphic hymns provide an intriguing glimpse at a mystery perhaps akin to the indigenous North American practice of praising the four directions. All of life is gathered in this pantheon of gods. Every aspect of human experience receives respect. The hymns are intended to perfect the world, to remind us of its sacredness and our own. Pythagoras was said to have coined the word *cosmos* to describe the coherence of the universe, a harmony that unites every element of it. Plotinus described this state of grace when he wrote: "The stars are like letters that inscribe themselves at every moment in the sky. Everything in the world is full of signs. All events are coordinated. All things depend on each other. Everything breathes together."

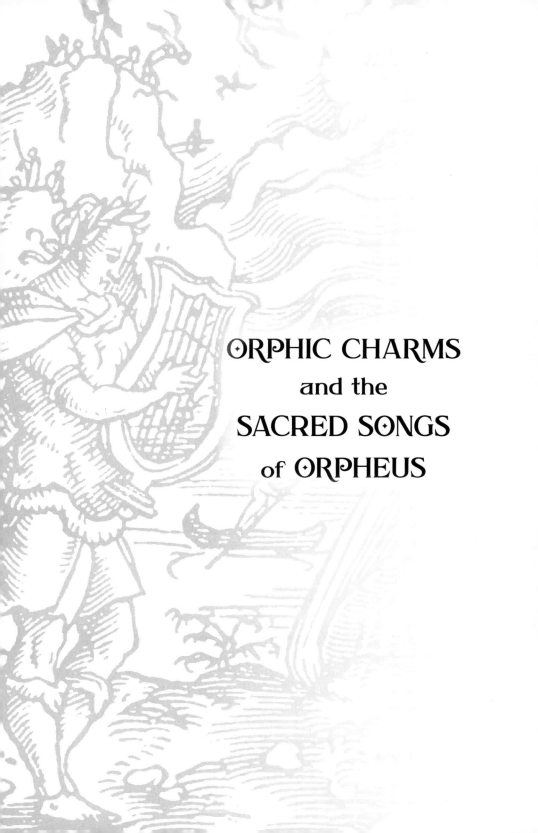

ORPHIC CHARMS
and the
SACRED SONGS
of ORPHEUS

Orphic Charms

These mysterious messages were hammered into gold leaf, sometimes in the shape of leaves. They are passwords for the dead, messages to avert forgetfulness. Except "Friend, Use it to Prosper," customarily titled "To Musaeus," which may have been a grand invocation, the commencement of an initiation, an instructional introduction, a prayer for the dead, or an all-around good luck charm.

Life Death Life
Truth

Orphic Fragment

Exploding from the Great Soul,
souls reel and writhe,
seeking each other in space.

From planet to planet we fall,
crying for home in the abyss,
we are your tears, Dionysus.

Mighty one! God of freedom!
Bring your children back into
your heart of singing light.

To the Left of the House of Hades

Under a graceful white cypress,
a well offers spring water
to refresh the descending dead.
Don't drink it!

Find the water flowing
From the lake of memory.
Guardians protect the cold water.
Tell them:

I am a child of earth
and of starry heaven,
but my race is of heaven.
This you know.

I am parched
and perishing.
Give me cold water
from the lake of memory.

They will give you water
from the sacred spring
and you will live
a lord among heroes.

The Well of Memory

I am parched with thirst—
dying.

Drink from me, the eternal spring
on the right by the cypress.
Who are you? They will ask.
Where are you from?

I am a child of earth
and starry heaven,
but my race is of heaven.

Hammered in Gold

When the spirit
has left the sunlight
then be wary of everything.

Hail, you who have suffered
the Suffering. This you
have never suffered before.

Once man
now God.

You are a kid
fallen in milk.

Hail, to you
walking on the right
by the sacred groves
and meadows of Persephone.

Cecilia's Golden Armor

She comes from the pure,
O pure Queen of the Dead.

Child of Zeus,
here is the armor
of memory:
a gift men love
to sing songs about.

For you, Cecilia Secundia,
to forever avert
the darkness of forgetfulness.

A Kid, I Have Fallen in Milk

Out of the pure I come.
Pure Queen of the Dead,
I am of your starry race.
I have paid the penalty
for unrighteous deeds.
Fate and the immortals
struck me with lightning
thrown from the stars.
I have flown away
from the weary wheel
of sorrows. Queen,
with eager feet
I come to your circle
in the heart of the underworld.
I ask mercy from Persephone,
that by her grace
she receive me
among the eternally blessed.

Magical Formula

Mix honey with milk,
drink the moment before dawn
to have something
holy in your heart.

Remember—
many pretend
few know.

Friend, Use It to Prosper

Hear this song,
know a sacred way.

Kind Zeus, and Gaia our earth,
pure fire of the sun,
holy light of the moon and every star,

Poseidon, shadowy earth belter,
pure Persephone,
and Demeter, mother of harvests,

arrow-pouring Artemis,
good Apollo who prophesies at Delphi,
and intoxicating Dionysus,
we honor you.

Ares quick to spill blood,
who desires only battlefields,
fiery Hephaistos,
sculptor and inventor,
sublime Aphrodite
risen from the sea,
and the King of the underworld,
we honor you.

Hebe, giver of youth,
Hercules, performer
of legendary labors,
Eileithyia the deliverer,
protector of birth,
opener of the gates to Earth,
we honor you.

The great blessings of Justice
and Faithfulness, beautiful Nymphs,
and musical Pan, lord of all,
we honor you.

We adore you, Hera, Queen of Heaven,
gracious Memory, and the sacred Muses.
Golden Leto, mother of Artemis
    and Apollo,
oracular Dione of Dodona, mother of
    Aphrodite,
we honor you.

Prophetic Kouretes, whose war dance
concealed Rhea as she bore Zeus.
Korybantes, who guarded Cybele
when she walked among lions.

Kabiri who gave us the Mysteries
in ancient Samothrace,
and the Dactyls on Mount Ida whose
    fingers
first worked metal in fire, we honor you.

Hermes, immortal messenger,
Themis, fair as nature,
primordial Night and Day, bringers of
    light,
saviors all, immortal children of Zeus,
we honor you.

Kronos of the golden age,
lord of the sickle of time,
Rhea, mother of the gods
in a chariot drawn by lions,

Thetis veiled in the blue deep,
mother of Achilles
and wife of Okeanos of the seven seas,
father of the Nymphs of the brine,
steady Atlas
shouldering the world,
unobstructed Eternity,
and ever-flowing Time,
we honor you.

The glistening water of the river Styx,
gentle gods all, Foresight,
Good Luck laughing in a vineyard,
Bad Luck the bane of all,
gods of the heavens and of the mist,
gods of all the waters,
gods on earth, under earth, and of fire,
we honor you.

Leukothea, goddess bright
as dawn-lit sea,
sister of amorous Semele,
mother of great Dionysus,
we honor you.

Palaimon, giver of bliss,
protector of ships,
inescapable Adresteia,
nemesis to injustice,
defender of the righteous,
nursemaid of Zeus,

honey-tongued Nike,
sweet Victory,
Asklepios the soothing,

Athena perfect warrior
and master of strategy,
we honor you.

The four winds, Thunder,
and everything under
the four-columned Cosmos,
we honor you.

The mother of the immortals,
Attis, bringer of spring,
the thirteen sisters Menae,
one for each lunar cycle,
we honor you.

She of Starry Heaven,
and sacred Adonis
immortal beauty,
the Beginning and the End,
we honor you.

Hear us with joy and mercy
our rite is holy
and our offerings sincere.

The Sacred Songs of Orpheus

According to tradition, Orpheus created these
sacred songs for his son Musaeus of Athens,
who wrote them down as his father
performed them.

Hecate

Terrifying Hecate
of the crossroads,
friend of the dead,
saffron-shrouded ghost
seen by barking dogs.

Queen of blackest night,
torch held high,
you walk beside Demeter
searching for Persephone.

You work from afar,
weaving spells of water, earth,
    sky, you catch
every eye in fatal trance.

Each night drawn by bulls of mist
you shine light across the sky.
Filled with your fire
stags rattle antlers.

Mother of sorcery and witchcraft,
of spells and superstitions,
you are the black puppy
and the black she lamb.
We offer you eggs and red fish.

Artemis, Opener of Ways

Eileithyia, you midwifed Zeus
at the birth of Athena.
Goddess of many names,
you are a sweet sight
to women in labor,
helpful to young mothers
you give easy births.

Gracious to all,
yours is the power
to nurture every house.
Delighted by celebrations
you loosen sashes.
Invisible, but seen in every action
you share in our pain
and rejoice in our births.
Eileithyia, free us
from suffering and sorrow.
Comfort our souls.
You alone give relief from pains of labor.
All we see around us you have brought
out of darkness into light.

Night

Nyx, mother of gods and men,
some call you Aphrodite.
Pitch-black, star-spangled goddess,
your children are our dreams.

You love celebrations.
We ask you to ease our worries,
give us rest from toil,
reward us with peaceful sleep.

Gleaming in darkness
you drive your black horses,
as you return to the underworld,
appearing then disappearing
from earth and sky.

You drench half our lives with darkness.
Your drowsy powers divide our days.
Necessity rules all,
yet you are who we call to dispel our fears.
Ancient Night, black-winged bird,
we honor you.

Sky

Father Sky, ruler of the stars
forever whirling around Gaia,
all worlds begin with you
and return to you,
hear us, most generous parent.

You guard the world
with the ever-enduring
laws of Necessity.

Harmonious universe,
home of gods and goddesses,
ever-changing infinity,
celestial but earthly azure
of the flux of forms,
no one can tame you.

All-seeing Sky,
father of Father Time,
forever shine your blessings upon us
inspire lives that are divine.

Light

Endless power and dwelling of Zeus,
to you belong the sun, moon, and stars.
Your fire tames all creatures.

Purest cosmic element,
light shining from the sun
and from countless stars,
without you there is no life
only darkness.
We honor you.

Guide us,
light that awakens life,
shine gently upon our orchards.
Bring warmth in the morning
and comfort us in the night.

Firstborn Revealer

Black-winged Night
loved the wind.
A silver egg was born.

Scattering dark mist from your eyes
your golden wings burst from the egg
shining pure light in all directions.

Cock at dawn
roaring bull
setting the world whirling.

Unforgettable seed
of all life, glorious sun,
firstborn father of gods and men,
guide us with your wisdom.

The Stars

Sky spirits
of purest light,
children of Night,
we honor you.

Dance circles
of far shining rays,
revealers of fate.

Suspended in space
you gaze upon luminous orbits.

Shining in Night's cloak of darkness,
indestructible in your blazing paths,
ripen us for works of honorable glory.

The Sun

First to reign over the gods
after your mother Night
on our world you shine light.

Self born each instant,
inexhaustible radiance,
sweet sight to all creatures,
we honor you.

You tune the seasons
as you guide your chariot
along your course.

Harsh to the wicked,
guide to the good,
strum your golden lyre
and illuminate our world.

Bless us with wisdom,
ever-shining health
and virtuous wealth,
ripener of harvests.

Moon

Splendid bringer of light,
bull-horned goddess Moon,
crossing the sky,
racing through night,
we honor you.

Stars attend your orbit
as you glide,
a torch in the darkness,
waxing and waning,
male and female.
We honor you.

Brooding amber
shining in the night,
all-seeing vigilance
in the sky of stars,
evening's splendor,
like a jewel you offer
fulfillment and favor.

In your long cloak of shadow
moving in circles,
you shepherd the Milky Way.
Holy and gentle lady of the stars,
let your light shine
and save us.

Nature

Resourceful all-mother,
goddess of abundance,
untamed all-tamer,
eternally glorious queen
of constantly unfolding creation,
men glorify you in fables,
seeing in the night
your imperishable light
the constellations.

We are all part of your
multitude of the unique.
Perpetual creativity,
you know us all.
Mother of flowers,
for love of you they twine.

Giver of life and nourishment,
you have many names.
You give the Graces
the power to persuade.

Magnificent giver of form,
motion of every movement,
source of every skill,
you command even kings.

Life everlasting, destined fate,
breath of life everywhere,
you alone do all these things.
We honor you.

Pan

Pan!
God of the wild universe,
of sky, sea, and earth,
eternal light
restlessly frolicking
with the Seasons,
you love frantic pleasure.

Weaver of universal harmony
in a playful song,
star-haunted goat,
you panic mortal minds
with terrifying delusions.

Gushing freshwater springs
delight you, friend of
shepherds and herdsmen,
dancer with Nymphs,
keen-eyed hunter.
Echo lover,

everything that grows
grows because of you.

Lord of the universe,
you have many names.
Zeus with horns, healer,
the power that turns a flower
into a fruit fully ripened.

You hold up the earth,
and the ocean that belts it,
the deep flowing waters
of the tireless sea,
the air that gives life
and the sublime eye
above of floating fire.
Each has a place in your harmony.
Your power changes every nature
as you nurture all.
We honor you.

Hercules

Strong-handed son of Zeus,
with the heart of a lion,
renowned for courageous action
and all-conquering energy,
help us.

Beyond words, lord of all,
everlasting, ever-changing,
all-conquering archer and seer,
devouring everything you create,
highest peak, helper to all,
you tame wild tribes, bringing
peace that nurtures children.
You bring shining honors.

You are the most brave of earth's sons,
illustrious healer, the gleam of dawn
and dark of dusk cling to you.
Your twelve heroic labors
span from east to west.

Irrepressible worldly immortal,
blessed charm against disease,
with your club drive misfortune away
and with your poisonous arrows
keep cruel death at bay.

Shake the tree,
give us a bite
of golden apple
for immortality.

Kronos

Eternal father
of immortals and mortals,
pure, mighty, resourceful,
you consume all
to nourish all.

Your unbreakable chains
bind everything to time.
We honor you.

Kronos, maker of spirals,
wily shifter of stories,
first child of earth and starry heaven,
in you we have birth and decline.

With one hand you give hope
and with the other cruelty.
You end struggle and suffering
but also contentment and love.

Revered source of foresight,
husband of Rhea the divine,
ancient root of all,
you are everywhere,
give a noble end to a good life.

Rhea

Daughter of many-faced Eros,
your chariot is drawn by
bull-slaying lions.

Furious frenzy of pounding
drums and clashing cymbals
delights you.

Mother of Zeus
who bears the aegis
of omnipotence,
blessed consort of Kronos,
wild mountains please you,
where the horrible shrieks
of your ecstatic priests
echo the din of war.

First mother
of immortals and mortals,
liar and savior, you gave
father Kronos a stone to eat
instead of Zeus
so our world could be born.
From you come the land,
the vast sky above,
the ocean and the winds.
We honor you.

Give us peace and wealth,
send death and the mud
of pollution far away
to the ends of the earth.

149

Zeus

The Bright One,
clear blue sky,
you were
you are
you will always be
supremely sacred Zeus.
We dedicate this to you.

Under the oak of Dodona
your prophet priests
with unwashed feet
crouch on the ground
listening to your voice
speaking softly in rustling
leaves and cooing doves.

We place before you
testimony in our favor.

You brought to light
divine Mother Earth,
hills swept by shrill winds,
oceans, and all the stars of the sky.

Strongest spirit, all father,
your scepter is a thunderbolt.
Beginning and end of everything,
you shake the earth.

Purify us. Give us increase.
Father of thunder and lightning
you are also Zeus the planter,
friend to farmers.

You are the law of hospitality,
the civility of privacy,
and respect for property.
We honor you.

The Milky Way,
the ladder of lights,
the path of souls,
we call the road of Zeus.

God of many faces,
grant perfect health,
blameless wealth,
sacred peace, and
honorable glory.

Hera

She of the heights,
we honor you.
In the dark
your soft breeze
nourishes mortal souls.

Queen of the Constellations,
ivory-armed wife of Zeus
who married you for love.
Goddess of sweet marriage,
protect mothers and children.

Glory of the eye of the peacock feather,
flowers bloom wherever you walk.
Without you nothing grows.
Grant us clear skies at favorable times.
Bless our fields with gentle rain.
Fierce protectress, shield us from strife,
we too are your children.

Poseidon

Earth belter,
the tides obey
your bronze trident.

From your dark mane
at the bottom of the sea
great waves flow.

Deep roaring ruler of oceans,
earth-shaker,
your flowers are waves
and your blossoms foam.

You urge your watery horses on
rushing and splashing
in the rippling brine.

You delight in the wild dwellers
under the waves, spirit of the deep.
We thank you for the gifts of the sea.

Protect our ships.
Give us tranquil harbors.
Keep the earth from quaking.
We honor you.

Hades

Subterranean Zeus,
you hold the keys
to everything earthly.
You give us the yearly wealth
of ripened fruit.
We honor you.

Your throne stands in moonless night,
in the dismal plain that stretches
from horizonless darkness to the same
where breathless specters roam
in the windless distance.

There you reign by the river Agony
where Gaia binds her roots to Fate.

Death obeys only you.
You receive us all,
master of mortals,

in muddy Tartarus,
the asphodel meadows,
or the Elysian Fields.

You took Demeter's daughter,
tore her from the meadow,
plunged her into the sea,
then through the gate to your realm
in the famous cave near Eleusis.

You were born to judge
our lives, the obvious and the secret.
Nothing is hidden from you.

Holiest most glorious ruler,
with respectful reverence
we ask for peace and favor,
for long life and blameless treasure.

Thundering Zeus

Ominous changes of weather
tell us you are near.
The rumble of your chariot
rolls through gathering gloom.

As you shake the earth,
wild animals cower,
eyes reflecting lightning,
as thunder fills the sky.

Bringer of storms and hurricanes
roaring like showers of arrows,
you light up everything
burning anything
so strong you make our hearts pound
as we feel our hairs stand on end.

Holy, invincible, sudden
endless spiraling din,
sound all devouring,
uncontrollable, threatening
storm crashing down
the column of water
dreaded on land and at sea.
Teach us to read your signs.
Protect our ships,
our flocks, fields, and orchards.
Give us strength and courage.
Guide us through unavoidable storms.
We honor you.

God of Lightning

Magnificent, pure,
glorious, resounding,
ethereal Zeus, your whip
blazes in the sky.

With a deafening crash
your winged fire thunders
light through the clouds,
swift as a diving eagle.
We honor you.

Frightening and invincible
lord of lightning,
all-father and highest king,
be kind and illuminate the path
to sweetness of life.

Clouds

Mothers of rain,
river traveling over
heaven's plain,
nourish our crops.

Wind-driven water bellies
full of thunder,
you conceal the sun,
the moon, the stars.

Story-telling shapes of the sky,
reflecting every fleeting color,
we honor you.

The Sea

Gray-eyed Tethys, bride of Ocean,
dark-veiled goddess of deep waters
blown to shore by sweet breezes,
your tall waves break on rocky beaches.

Calm, gentle, smooth,
you are the delight of ships,
mother of rivers whose waters
quench the thirst of wild creatures.

Mother of Aphrodite,
of darkening clouds,
and freshwater springs,
the playgrounds of Nymphs,
we honor you.

Send a fair wind to fill our sails.
Bless us with the bounty of the sea.

Nereus

Old man of the sea,
in blue-black darkness
fifty beautiful Nymphs,
your daughters,
dance gracefully
in the currents.
We honor you.

Ocean of life,
where everything began,
you make the earth tremble
when you lock storm winds
in your gloomy deep.

Venerable watcher,
fish-tailed shape-shifter,
savior of sailors,
teacher of Aphrodite,
prophet gentle, truthful,
and merciful, eternal
friend to mortals,
save us from chaos.

The Nereids

Daughters of Nereus,
you live in the golden castle
at the bottom of the sea.
Your steeds are Tritons,
the mermen with wings.
You delight in the creatures
of the billowing brine.

Long hair flowing
in the deepest water,
you ride seahorses
and glistening dolphins
as you roam the roaring waves.

You first showed us
the sacred rites of Dionysus
and of pure Persephone,
you and great Apollo,
and Calliope, leader of the Muses,
inspirer of poets and kings.
We honor you all.

Beautiful Nymphs,
save us from death by water.
Let only the lake of memory
quench our thirst.

Proteus

Firstborn,
by your power
the acorn becomes
a mighty oak.

Changing intricate matter
you elaborate life
into endless shapes,
god of rivers.

You know what is,
what was, and what will be.
We honor you.

Transforming more than
the immortals of snowy Olympus,
you soar over land and sea
through the air and all nature.

Shepherd of the sea
you doze with your colony
of seals on sand warm as
the sun of the Nile Delta.

Reluctant oracle,
only to those who capture and hold you
through all your transformations
do you reveal your clear prophecies.

Protect us, we are your children.
Give us long and blameless lives.

Earth

Gaia divine mother
of immortals and mortals,
you nourish us all,
you give all,
you ripen everything,
you destroy everything,
creator of all you devour.

First bride at the first wedding,
in spring, heavy with fruit
and blossoming flowers,
you give birth everywhere
to beings who revere you,
seed of the eternal universe.

You are the pure pulse
in everything: vast, eternal, deep.
Yours is the breath of sweet grass
and the joy of rain.
Goddess of flowers,
we honor you.

From the sky all around you
stars gaze at your perfection.
Blessed goddess,
increase our harvests.
With your companions,
the sublime Seasons,
show us favor.

The Mother of the Gods

Most-honored mother of immortals,
nurturer of us all,
bull-killing lions
draw your chariot,
Queen of the Sky,
hear our prayers.

Mother of Zeus,
we pound drums, clash shields,
crash cymbals, and dance
to celebrate you.

Daughter of starry heaven,
beloved of Kronos,
you are Rhea and Cybele.
The first mother
and mother of us all,
we honor you.

Care for us
raise us
protect us.
Nurture your children.

Hermes

Messenger of Zeus,
son of mother Maia,
your grandfather Atlas
shoulders the world,
Hermes, subtle and clever,
kindly judge our competitions.

Guide of the dead,
you lulled then killed
hundred-eyed Argos
to give the peacock
beautiful feathers.
We honor you,
child who made Apollo's lyre.
Doorways, roads,
and borders amuse you.
You love secrets, tricks,
gambling, and gymnastics.

Gracious sage,
good shepherd,
trusted guardian,

on winged sandals
you fly between worlds.
Free us from worry,
lover of prophets
and profits.

Interpreter of all,
in your hand you hold
the pure instrument of peace.
Your gifts are casually found treasures.

God of the fickleness
of thought and speech,
friend to thieves and liars,
protect us from them.

With the touch of your wand
you bring dreams,
sleep, or death.
We honor you,
guide us through
this world and the next.

Persephone

Where are you, Persephone,
in the darkness of winter?
In moonlit meadows of early spring
your crown of asphodel flowers
glows like constellations.

Wife of Hades,
daughter of Zeus,
and only child of Demeter,
you command the dismal gates
deep in the earth
that separate the living from the dead.

Blossom of rebirth,
glory of spring,
mother of Dionysus
and the Furies,
giver of harvests,
we honor you.

In spring you are the joy
of blooming apricot trees.
We see your sacred beauty
in fresh shoots and ripe fruit.

Bride of an abductor,
you were a virgin
walking in a field
collecting flowers
when Hades saw you
and took you away.

Your mother searched
everywhere for you.
She found you
in the underworld.

Persephone,
because you ate
pomegranate seeds
at the table of Hades,
Zeus decreed
you spend six months
every year underground.
Your absence we call winter.

When you return
to wander smiling

in sunlit fields,
your footsteps and voice
awaken spring.

Our footsteps lead to the realm
you rule with mighty Hades.
Until then give us gentle-handed
    health
and blameless wealth.
Show us how to live well
so we will not fear your judgment.

Guide us out of winter.
Show us again
the bountiful revival.

Persephone
of the beautiful ankles
and aspen hair,
you are the star
at the core of the apple.

Dionysus

Roar loud and celebrate!
Dionysus! Primal,
of two natures,
born three times!
Face of the mighty bull,
vigorous as ivy,
howler in battle,
we honor you.

Broad leaves of the wild
wrap you, clusters of grapes
adorn you, son of the forbidden
love of Zeus for Persephone.

With the rain Nymphs of Nysa
who nourished you,
intoxicate us
with the sacredness of wilderness.

Kouretes

Leaping to the sound
of weapons crashing,
roaring warriors swarming
like bees around hives
on wild mountainsides,
you pound the ground
with nimble feet,
striking swords to shields
to hide the cries
of mother then child
at the birth of Zeus
in danger from his father.
We honor you,
protect us!

Athena

Born fully armored
from the head of Zeus,
you love swords, spears, and shields.
All powerful and terrifying dignity,
inspire us to bravery.

You dart like a swallow
in still meadows
in mountain shadows
from caves to windy hilltops
and in the rafters
when the hero returned
to fight for his wife and throne.

Mother of all arts,
we honor you.
You have never answered
the call to love's alluring bed.

You prefer the clash of weapons
so you drive our souls to madness.
Owl-eyed spear-shaker
swift war winner,
shrewd counselor
and shape-shifter,
destroyer of the hundred-handed giants
who dared rebel against the gods.

Gray-eyed goddess,
we honor you.
You gave Athens
her olive trees
and the golden words
that gilded Greece.
Lead us and guide us
to heroic victories.

Nike

Omnipotent Victory,
in the palm of Athena's hand
you stand, wings outstretched.

Desired by everyone,
only you can free us
from strife of competition
and the terrors of war.

You judge the hero,
you grant the prizes,
no boast is sweeter
than your favor.
We honor you.

You rule all.
From your good name comes glory,
born from battle
but bright with celebration.
In your chariot you appear
at every hero's side
to give the laurel crown
of fame and renown.
Grant us the greatest victory.

Apollo

When Python attacked your mother
as you were waiting
in her womb to be born,
you did not forget.
When you became a full-grown god,
like the sun you appeared
on the peak of Parnassus where
only beams of light can reach.
You chased Python back to Delphi,
where you claimed the oracle
that had belonged to Gaia.
With your shining arrows
you ended the reptile's life.

Yours are the lyre,
the seed and the plow.
Wild light-bringer,
glorious youth,
lovable immortal,
your arrows fly far.

Leader of the dance of the Muses,
holy one, slayer of vermin,
your ambiguous oracle
deceives the deceitful with truth.
For the virtuous
your prophecies are clear.

You see everything,
bringing light to all beings,
hear with heartfelt kindness
prayers for the people.

You gaze always
upon the fertile earth,
even at twilight.
Upon the arrival of the stars
in the reflection of the moon
you shine upon us.
We honor you.

You watch the roots of earth
as you hold the limits of the world
and make all lives harmonize
with the chords you strum.
Every beginning is yours
and every end.
Your music is the sound
of everything blooming.

You give the races of living beings
our natures and differences
as you harmonize every fate,

giving equal measures
of winter and summer,
striking low notes in winter
and the highest in summer.

Always everywhere
you give subtle advice
through oracles, dreams,
and bird flight.
Teach us the science
of harmony and limits.

Tune winter's dour strings
to spring's sweetness.
Strike summer's purest chord.
Play autumn's hymn of harvest.

Let the wind song
of the syrinx sing
a dance for Pan.

Yours is the seal
that gives forms
to the cosmos.
Hear us and save us.

Leto

Dark-veiled Night,
mother of the twin lights
to whom many pray.
You suffered the birth pangs
of Zeus's bright children,
the sun and the moon.
We honor you.

Ortygia, isle of the quail,
which had floated free,
for you Zeus fixed
to the bottom of the sea.
There great Artemis was born.
Under the shining peak of Delos
by the rushing stream
and the sacred pool,
in the shade of palm and laurel,
you gave birth to shining Apollo,
under the watchful gaze
of your sister Asteria,
goddess of the stars.

Hear us, Leto,
bless all our beginnings.

Asteria

Deathless Titan,
mother of Hecate,
to escape Zeus
you threw yourself
like a falling star
into the boiling sea.

You became Ortygia,
isle of the quail,
and its sacred city Delos,
where your sister Leto
gave birth to Artemis and Apollo,
twin lamps of the sky.

You inspire prophetic dreams,
star reading, messages between
the living and the dead,
and all oracular arts of the night.

We honor you,
illuminate our lives.

Artemis

You have many names,
daughter of Zeus.
Revered archer,
with your torch you bring
light to us all.

In the mountains of eastern Crete
they call you Diktynna
of the Dancing Plants.

Helper of labor
you will never know,
virgin, huntress,
fire your arrows
and drive our worries away.

You are the moon
roaming the wilds.
Redeemer, fame-bringer,
nurturer of the young,
immortal, yet earthly.

Your realms are the forests
and mountains where hounds
love to run with you when you hunt.
For you girls with pine torches
dance around laurel trees.

Hear us, savior,
banish pain and disease
to the most distant
mountain peaks.
Give us uninterrupted peace.

The Titans

Glorious children of sky and earth,
ancestors of our fathers,
you dwell deep underground.

From you comes every toiling creature,
mortals of the sea and of the land,
the birds, and all the ephemeral
generations of the world.

Drive out cruel anger.
If some unknown forefather
stormed your homes
forgive innocent descendants.

The Kouretes

Bronze-clashing
priests of Ares,
bodies of sky,
earth and seas,
send the life-nurturing breeze.

Glorious saviors,
protectors of sailors,
you were the first
to teach us the sacred mysteries.
We honor you.

Driven by you
oceans crash
against shores.
Dust from your march
reaches the clouds.
Your pounding feet
shake the forest
as your armor gleams
flashing in the sky.
Wild animals cower
at your onslaught
as your shouts
fill the heavens.

Immortals, you nurture,
and you destroy.
Fretting angrily over us,
you ruin our crops
and scatter our herds.
As storms groan
ancient trees fall uprooted.

Celestial twins of Olympus,
breathe gently upon us.

Korybas

Great king of immortal earth,
blessed Korybas, fierce as Ares
whom no one can oppose.

Ruler of the nocturnal Koretes,
roamer of deserted places,
help us avoid danger
when we are panicked
by ghosts or delusions.

Divine male and female,
you take many shapes
stained red with blood,
murdered by your quarreling brothers.

The mother of the gods decreed
that you transform your purified body
into the black dragon
we call upon to protect us.

Hear us, rejoice in our song,
protect us from anger's grief.
Banish the phantoms
our fears create
when Necessity terrifies us.

Demeter

Goddess all-mother
of many names,
revered nurturer
of every youth,
pure mother bee,
giver of wealth,
nourisher of corn,
you love peaceful hard work.

Watch over the sowing,
the harvest and the threshing.
Ripener of orchards,
we honor you.

You dwell in holy solitude
in the valley of Eleusis,
fascinating beauty
nourishing all mortals.
Your gentle wisdom
first yoked ox to plow.

Green of every leaf,
up from below the ground,
you raise our harvests.
Mother of summer,
you are how we all grow.
You make every bud bloom.

Let your glorious torch
shine joy upon the colorful brood
of children, cubs, and flowers.

Demeter Antaia

Shining-haired daughter of the stars,
mother of immortals and mortals,
sender of visions at night,
we honor you.

Weary searcher far and wide,
grieving wanderer
accompanied by apparitions,
your anger made barren the earth.
Great Mother, save us from famine.
Depriving the gods of sacrifice,
you opposed all, hostile to life,
until you drank water,
barley meal and pennyroyal
in the valley of Eleusis
where you began your journey
to rescue Persephone.

The innocent child
guiding you brought news
of the sacred wedding
of subterranean Zeus.

Every mortal meets you
on the road taken by all.
Guide us as we travel.
Hear our need
and give good counsel,
graciously notice the humble.

Mise

Female Dionysus,
divine lawgiver
of many names,
a pinecone-tipped
stalk of fennel
wrapped in ivy
is your scepter.

Unforgettable wisdom
of good counsel,
holy ineffable
female and male,
hear us.

You delight in
your mother's rites
in elegant Eleusis,

wild Phrygia,
and lovely Cyprus

on plains of wheat fields,
and by the flooding Nile
where your revered mother,
black-robed Isis, reigns.

As rain and ocean Nymphs
tend your every need,
with kindness view
our initiation games.

Approve our holy rites,
reward reverence
with seasons ideal
for ripening fields.

The Seasons

Daughters of Zeus
and the Titan Themis,
goddess of justice
and the balances,
we honor you.
Teach us nature's laws.

Always blooming,
ever-turning Seasons,
your robes are the dew
on flourishing flowers
as you accompany
the Fates and the Graces
when Persephone
comes out to the light.

Notice our holy rites,
reward reverence
with seasons ideal
for making fields ripe.

Semele

Mother of joyous Dionysus,
shining-haired daughter
of Kadmos, old man of the east,
father of the city of Thebes
who brought the alphabet to Greece,
Zeus loved you so
he granted you any wish.

You asked to see his splendor.
In agony you died
by the fiery thunderbolt
of the immortal's unveiled glory.

Every third year, Persephone
honors you, allowing you
to attend the sacred rites,
for every mortal reenacts
your sacred ritual
of the holy mysteries
of unveiled light.

Dionysus in the Fox Skin

Son of the thunderbolt,
master of everything,
you have many names.
Face of the bull,
bloody swords delight you.

Joining in the revelry of the howling
frenzy of your sacred Maenads,
the raving ones, you roar
from Mount Nysa to Mount Olympus.

Save us from your wrath,
intoxicating immortal
with your scepter
of ivy, pine, and fennel,
all the gods and men
inhabiting earth honor you.

Leaping ecstasy
of immortality
give joy to all.

Dionysus in the Cradle

Born in the mountains
of faraway Nysa
where pine and cinnamon
perfume the breeze,
joy of flowers,
you are their power to bloom.
We honor you.

Nursling of Maenads and Muses,
Aphrodite's fairest petal,
she too watched over you.
You compel the Nymphs
to quiver in dance
in the frenzy of your grace,
making the forests feel your feet.

Wise Zeus guided you
to noble Persephone
who raised you to be adored.
Looking into your eyes,
even gods know awe.
With kind heart
accept our rites.

Dionysus Twined around the Pillar

You give grape seeds
power to break dirt.
You ripen to bleed
on the wine press.
We honor you.

When thunderbolts blaze
and gales rage,
when mountains quake,
twine your vines
around our pillars.

Mighty Dionysus,
make our house strong
as you did for Kadmos
who brought writing
from Phoenicia to Thebes.
With joyous heart
bless this celebration.

Sabazius

On the mountain in Anatolia
where Tmolos, son of Ares,
judged the music of Apollo and Pan,
you, illustrious Zeus,
son of Kronos,
in your sewn-up thigh
saved baby Dionysus
until he could be born.

There Hipta of the fair cheeks,
his wet nurse,
the soul of the universe,
cared for you both.
Great god of the near east,
we honor you.
With heartfelt kindness
hear us and protect us.

Dionysus

Son of Zeus and Persephone,
your father set you on his throne,
his thunderbolts in your hands.

But the Titans distracted you
with toys and mirrors.

When they attacked, you changed forms
many times until you became the bull
they stabbed and devoured.

Immortal who died
to be born again,
protect us.

Hipta

Nursemaid of Dionysus,
mother of secret rites
choruses sing
by crackling fires,
you saw the Titans
butcher Dionysus.

They boiled him first
then roasted him.
Zeus destroyed them
with thunderbolts.
From the bloody ashes
we were born.

When we hunger for revenge,
when we measure envy,
serve chaos, and surrender to frenzy
of blood-drenched bronze,
sweet wet nurse who
witnessed our birth,
comfort and protect us.
We honor you.

Dionysus the Liberator

Bacchus of the wine,
treasure of many names,
spirit who saves us,
holy son of Zeus you were
secretly born from two mothers.

Plump giver of countless joys
and of good fruit,
you break earth
and grow to fill the wine press
with healing for our pain.

Holy flower,
hating sorrow,
like vines your tresses curl.
Spirit of celebration,
your pine-cone-tipped
ivy-wound fennel stalk
inspires ecstasy.
Save us, Dionysus,
ripener of grapes.
We honor you.

The Nymphs

Daughters of Ocean,
dwellers in the dark
damp caverns of Earth,
as secret as the paths you take,
nursemaids of Dionysus,
haunters of mist and meadows,
playful and natural
as pollen-dusted bees
sipping nectar.

You love winding roads
and deep grottos.
Quick, agile, dewy,
you love to wander,
dancing with Pan
through remote valleys,
humming like bees
among the flowers,
or gliding down rocks
on the mountainside.

Girls of the fields,
of gushing freshwater springs,
sweet smelling as wildflowers,

protectors of goat herds,
pastures, and orchards,
even wild animals adore you.

Delicate yet delighted by cold,
spring's first seedlings
sunlit in melting snow,
you feed us all
and help us grow.

Spirits of the trees,
playing in water
in joy of spring,
healers, you walk
with Dionysus
and the all-mother.

Pour pure rain
on our thirsty crops.
Give us grace
and joyful hearts.
We honor you.

To the God of the Feast of
Every Other Year

Bull-horned immortal,
Dionysus, God of Mount Nysa,
friend of many names,
lead our procession of torches
through the night,
dance in celebration
the frenzy that gives serenity.

Son of two mothers,
in your fawn skin
you explore the wilderness
of moonlit mountains.

Newborn crowned with ivy
in a cradle of grapes,
show us how to be reborn,
god who liberates.

To the God of the Yearly Feast

Wake,
sleeper in Persephone's hall,
time slumbers with you
as winter freezes all.

Wake
for the sacred feast.
Wake
the wild-haired Nymphs sleeping at
    your feet.
They will dance and sing
the ecstasy of life.

Wake,
Dionysus who gave us the vine.
Accept this milk and incense.
With joy give abundant fruit,
sacred and perfectly ripened.

Silenos

Second father of Bacchus,
greatest of the elder satyrs,
honored by immortals
and by mortals at the feast
of every other year,
we honor you.

Leader of the pastoral procession
of sleepless celebration,
bring the ivy-crowned Nymphs
of freshwater springs,
fountains, and streams.

Bring the howlers, the satyrs.
half-man half-goat spirits
of the wilderness and fields,
and all celebrants,
mortal and immortal.

Reveal the sacred
by torchlight sing and shout
the holy litany until tranquility
transforms our ceremony.

Aphrodite

Aphrodite of the heavenly smile,
many hymns praise you.

Born from the sea-foam,
goddess of creation,
you love all celebrations.
You bring lovers together at night.

Mother of Necessity, your sway
holds the world together.
We honor you.

You create us all,
everything in the sky,
everything on the fruitful land,
everything in the ocean deep.

Wise friend of Bacchus,
lover of festivities,
fresh as a bride,
mother of Eros,
goddess Persuasion,
whose joy is love's bed.

Mysterious giver of grace,
beautiful-haired daughter

of the starry heavens,
bridal feast companion
of the immortals,
beloved lover,
followed by fawning wolves
and cooing doves,
giver of birth and life.

Your love charms
harness mortals with madness.
You release the uncontrolled passions
of every race of beasts.
You are beautiful necessity
even in the frenzy of the shark.

Delicate as sea-foam of Cyprus,
fragrant as Syrian oils,
bright as golden chariots
on Egyptian plains
by the sandy bank
of the turquoise Nile,
a choir of the loveliest Nymphs
sings a hymn to your beauty.

Goddess of Cyprus
are you on Mount Olympus?
Are you riding your swan-drawn chariot

over the waves of the sea,
joining the creatures of the deep
in their dancing circles?

Are you at the beach
where your dark-faced Nymphs
frolic with light feet in the sand?

Are you in Cyprus where they cherish you,
as lovely virgins and chaste brides
praise you all year long,
singing of immortal Adonis?

Hear these sacred words,
beautiful goddess, and bless us.

Adonis

Hear us, god of many names,
we honor you!

In the solitude filled with song,
many-shaped friend and nurturer,
forever fresh bloom,
you are both male and female,

Adonis, when you vanish
we who love you weep
until spring returns.

Joyful hunter,
sweet blossom,
lover of Aphrodite,
born on the bed
of Persephone.

Deep in muddy Tartarus
you dwell, then on Olympus.
Doomed to set,
you rise in glory.
Laughter follows tears.

For you the women of Athens
plant seeds in broken pots

then leave the sprouts to die
on the roof in the sun
as they mourn your death
in what they call your gardens.

Blessed one, bring us
abundance of harvests.
Every year we celebrate your birth
and mourn your demise.
Notice our sacred rites.

Hermes Guide of Souls

On the road of no return
all mortals take,
by the river of weeping,
you guide souls
to the underworld.

Hermes, loved by Aphrodite,
the goddess worshipped long ago
in the oldest city of Cyprus,
we honor you.

Guide from horizon to horizon,
doomed mortals you bring
to the fated harbor.

With your sacred wand
you charm souls with sleep
then wake them again.

Persephone gave you
the great responsibility
of leading the way
to the place beyond life.

Bless our works,
guide us well,
lead our souls.
to the perfect meadow.

Love

Holy and pure Eros,
winged archer,
you play with the passions
of immortals and mortals alike.

Inventive, androgynous
master of everything,
of celestial light,
of the creatures of the roaring waves,
of all that dwell in the underworld,
on the earth and in the sky,
of all the creative winds
that carry seeds of grass
and grain for the goddess
who nourishes mortals.

You alone control
every course.
Bring us pure thoughts
and banish vile urges
that lead not to joy but to ruin.
Ennoble the devoted
with your glory.

The Fates

In the shadow
of the deepest cave,
warm darkness melts ice
freeing a fountain that streams
through barren rock.
It travels far
to feed the lake
you sit beside,
daughters of Night.

You have power over all.
Elated men, who forget
they are born to decay,
ride the fatal plain
with opinion for a guide
while you keep secret
the limits of hope
in dark purple,
inaccessible,
beyond Justice,
anxious Faith,
ancient Law,

or the measureless
power of Order.
The Fates alone watch
every life. The other
immortals of Olympus
seldom if ever notice us,
except for Zeus
whose perfect sight
knows all things
for all time.

Kindly hear us,
Klotho who spins the thread,
Lakhesis who measures it,
Atropos who cuts.

Relentless, invincible
Necessity, you give all
and take all.
We honor you.

The Graces

Glorious daughters
of Zeus and Eunomia,
she who gave order to the Seasons.

Aglaia, grace of splendor,
Thalia, loveliness of celebration,
and joyous Euphrosyne.
Beautiful, wise, pure
mothers of happiness
blooming everywhere,
you take many forms
adored by mortals.
We honor you.
Ever gentle, reveal
the blessings of beauty.

Nemesis

Great goddess,
your all-seeing eye
watches every race.
Immortal, we revere
you, rejoice in justice.
You see our thoughts
churning without rest
and you change them.
Mortals everywhere
groan under the burden
of your judgment.

The arrogant and reckless
find no escape.
You see everything,
you hear all,
you judge everyone.
Sublime goddess,
you are justice,
avenge the innocent.

Justice

Piercing eye of Zeus,
you see everything.
You crush the wicked
with righteous vengeance.

You are waiting for everyone
in the place where punishments
for forgotten crimes are assigned.

To the just you are gentle.
Notice our noble thoughts,
and with soft hands guide
and guard our lives.
Beautiful goddess,
we honor you.

Equality

Ideal of justice to mortals,
blessed and adored,
honored by all,
bold and lofty,
pure of thought,
you give us dignity
and decency.

We love to celebrate you,
charm of joyous peace,
as we strive for happy lives.

The unjust disgust you,
but you love the just.
In you the wisdom of virtue
reaches its most noble end.
We honor you.

Hear us, goddess
of the balance and cornucopia,
inspire us to serve you,
help us be worthy of your blessings.

Law

Sacred ruler of immortals
and mortals, order
that arranges the stars,
you give earth and ocean
their proper places.
Your rule steadies
nature's balance.

Law, loyal friend
to virtuous thoughts,
we honor you.

Guide our course,
primordial wisdom,
bring peace to our homes.

Give us honorable wealth
and lifelong health.
Preserve the civility, safety,
and unity of our community.

Number

You describe, identify,
and define all things.
You are the beautiful order
of our universe,
the logic of our grammar.

You are ratio,
rank, proportion,
perspective.

By your power
matter divides
and multiplies,
the One becomes many,
the many become One.

Teach us secrets
of harmony and measure,
the music of the architecture
of a life well lived.

Ares

Indestructible will,
spirit of might,
you love weapons.
Unconquerable
slayer of men,
you turn walls to rubble.
Holy Ares,
yours are the horrid sounds of war.

Blood splattered,
you enjoy killing.
In the chaos of battle,
your music is the clash of weapons.

Stop rage, end strife,
ease your painful grip on life.
Dionysus is giving a party.
Surrender to Aphrodite.
Put down your mighty sword,
for the sake of the Great Mother
who longs for peace.
We honor you.

Hephaistos

Inexhaustible fire,
you shine in every flame.
Bringer of light to mortals,
we honor you.

Inventive element most sublime,
the sun, the moon, the stars,
our campfires, candles, and lamps
are imitations of your glory.

Every home, city, and state
belongs to you, powerful
giver of blessings.
You dwell in the heat
of our living bodies.

Hear this sacred song
and listen gently to our joy.
Purify us
with a steady flame.

Asclepius

Second only to Apollo,
healer of all,
your music charms away
the pain of those who suffer.
We honor you.

Your soothing power
gives cures in dreams,
driving away threatening death.

Holy spirit of happiness,
helper who banishes evil,
enemy of sickness,
honored and mighty
son of Apollo,
hear us and save us.

Hygeia

Most-honored Queen,
charming as clear morning,
blessed all-mother,
bliss-bringer, hear us.

You make the sickness
that afflicts us vanish.
You make every home
blossom with joy.
We honor you.

When the world celebrates you,
Queen, every art thrives.

Hades, reaper of souls,
resents you for delaying
the increase of his kingdom.

You taught us that cleanliness prevents
    harm.
You gave us the key to making each
    day new.
Keep away the unbearable
distress of sickness.
Grace us with shining health.

The Furies

Daughters of Earth and shadow,
children of Night,
revered goddesses,
hear us.

Tisiphone, avenger of murder,
mother of retaliation.

Allekto whose anger never ends,
the pain inflictor
we fear to name;

terrifying Megaira
mother of crisis,
mother of grudges.

The wicked schemes of mortals
infuriate you. Rabidly righteous
you howl over Necessity's judgments
in the dank cavern by the hated holy
    river Styx.

You cause the agony of retribution.
Your realm is Hades where,
dog-headed, snake-haired,

draped in gray, you see every
moment of our lives as
your red eyes search
the newly dead passing by.

Airy phantoms, invisible
and swift as thought,
the speeding rays of the sun
and the glowing moon
cannot make life delightful
without your approval.

Snake-haired yet many-shaped
goddesses of Fate,
you guard the sacred order,
the course of the sun,
the superiority of wisdom.

You gaze upon the countless
races of all mortals
with the eye of Justice.
We honor you.
Protect us from harm.

The August Goddesses

Hear us, graciously and kindly,
pure daughters of subterranean Zeus
and fair Persephone, we honor you.

You carefully watch the wicked.
With the power of Necessity
you punish the unjust.

Until that time
when snake-haired Fate
summons us to holiness,
show us how to live good lives.

Melinoe

Saffron-cloaked,
nymph of Earth,
Persephone gave birth to you
on the sacred bed of Zeus
by the mouth of the wailing river.

Disguised as Hades
Zeus tricked Persephone,
his wily scheme seduced her.
From Persephone's fury sprang
an apparition with two bodies
that drives mortals mad.

Melinoe, your phantoms in the air
unnerve us in the nightly gloom.
You appear in strange shapes
and eerie forms, now shadowy,
then visible shining in the dark.

Inspire us to live blameless lives
and chase away our fears.
We honor you.

Fortuna

Notice our prayers,
Tyche, glorious Queen,
gentle goddess of roads.
Grant us plenty.

Giver of good counsel,
your wish is irresistible.
Our lives are the destiny you bestow.

Men blame you because
to some you give plenty
but others receive only poverty.

Wheel of fortune,
rudder of fate,
let our city be your crown.
We honor you.

Hear us, goddess,
kindly notice our piety,
and from your cornucopia
give us joy and renown.

Spirit

Gentle Zeus,
awe inspiring,
source of everything,
you give mortals life.
We honor you.

Avenger, ruler of all,
you are everywhere.
When you enter a house
your abundant powers
refresh the lives of mortals
worn out by work.

Yours are the keys
to joy and sorrow.
Banish painful worries
and the cares that cause
ruin to all the living.
Let honorable lives
receive peaceful ends.

Leukothea

White goddess we revere,
Ino, fair daughter of Kadmos,
bright as ocean salt,
wet nurse of Dionysus, hear us.

You love deep water,
delighting in waves.
Savior of mortals,
every ship at sea
with each unsteady heave
depends on you.

You rescue men
from horrid drowning,
swiftly you arrive.
Our welcome savior,
we honor you.

Goddess, help us,
save our sailors
and our ships.
Send fair winds
to fill our sails.

Palaimon

Friend of joyful Dionysus
dancing in celebration,
we honor you.

You live in the restless
pure ocean depths.
Your father killed your brother
then chased you
with your mother Ino
off a cliff into the sea.

Remembering she
wet-nursed Dionysus,
Zeus made you both immortal.

Friends of the dolphins,
when storms strike
our sea-roving ships,
rescue us
from the cruel cold
of the surging brine.

The Muses

Daughters of Memory
and thundering Zeus,
famous and illustrious,
you take many shapes.

Beloved by the mortals you visit,
from you comes pure inspiration.
Nourish our souls,
set our hearts alight,
guide us.

You taught us mystic rites,
goddesses of pure springs.
Beautiful-voiced Calliope,
inspire epic poetry.
Cleo, tell us history.
Erato, awaken love.
Euterpe, inspire music.
Melpomene, tell tragedy.
Terpsichore, show us dance.
Thaleia, give us comedy.
Ourania, inspire astronomy.

Polyhymnia, muse we depend
upon for our sacred hymns,
inspire our poetry.

No desire is stronger
than love of your light.
Hear us, goddesses
diverse and holy,
inspire us to honor your glory.

Memory

Consort of Zeus,
you gave birth to the sacred
clear-voiced Muses.
We honor you.

Oblivion harms minds
but not yours, giver of coherence
to the souls of mortals.

Sweet, vigilant, you remind us
of all the thoughts we store
forever in our hearts.

You are the remorse we feel
when we learn what we have done.
Yet you allow us to visit again
all the sweetness we have known.
You dissolve time to make us smile
even while sorrows moan.

With these powers you teach us
to understand the difference
between right and wrong.

Help us recall
who we are
and where we come from.

Blessed goddess,
help us remember
these sacred rituals,
keep them forever.

Dawn

You bring daylight to mortals,
glorious Dawn, you glide over the world
as messenger of the illustrious sun.
Night retreats wherever you arrive.
We honor you.

Your saffron sky delights us.
No one escapes your sight
as you watch from above,
chasing sleep from every eye.

You are joy for all mortals,
animals, birds, from
seeds to trees
and the broods of the sea,
where even fish rejoice
in the rebirth of color.
You blush rose splendor
on every horizon.

Themis

Daughter of the Sky,
flower of the Earth,
lovely young maiden,
first prophetess to show us
the holy oracle of the gods
in the sanctuary of Delphi
where Python was king.

You taught great Apollo
the art of lawmaking.
You taught our ancestors
morality and hospitality.
We revere and honor your
light in the darkness
for you were the first
to teach mortals how to worship.

Holder of the balances,
you are the glory of the gods
and of the sacred mysteries.
Divine order, good counsel,
hear us with kindness and joy
and bless our sacred rites.

North Wind

Boreas, wintry blast
from snowy Thrace,
you make the heavens tremble.

Disperse the rebellious
alliance of clouds and sleet,
hurry the storm
to bring fair weather
everywhere.

Brighten the face of the sky,
let the sun shine upon us.
We honor you.

Zephyr

Sea breeze from the west,
ethereal miracle,
refreshed workers
smile at your softness
when you cross the ocean
to fill meadows
with quiet sounds.

Oceanus sends you
to refresh the dead heroes
in the Elysian Fields.

Son of Dawn,
adored by harbors,
ships cut smooth
when you fill sails
with your soft breeze.
We honor you.
Grace us, be generous
with your gentle breath.

South Wind

Notos, your wings whip the wet air
as you ride the southern clouds.
We honor you.

Zeus gave you this honor,
to bring from sky to earth
the harvest nourishing downpours.

For this we pray, holy one,
that delighted by our rite
you will refresh Mother Earth.

Oceanus

Ageless ocean,
father eternal
of immortals and mortals,
your waves set
the boundaries of our shores.

From you come all seas,
every river, the pure flow
of freshwater springs.
We honor you.

Your currents carry ships
to the ends of the earth.
Hear us, divine purifier,
grace us with your favor.

Hestia

Daughter of great Kronos,
firstborn, sister of Zeus,
mistress of the eternal flame,
your fire warms every home.
With this sacred ritual raise us.

Many-shaped immortal,
keeper of the hearth of the gods,
mighty support of us all,
holy one, we honor you,
kindly accept our offering.

You are the power that bakes bread.
Soften necessity with domesticity,
goddess of shelter and family,
of community and continuity.
When we meet darkness
let your hearth warm every home.

Sleep

Master of all
immortals and mortals,
of every life
the vast earth nurtures,
you visit us
binding our bodies
with chains never forged.

Freeing us from worries
you offer sweet rest from toil.
We honor you.

Giving sacred comfort to every
    sorrow,
save souls, since you are the true
    brother
of Oblivion and Death.

We ask, sweet Hypnos,
be our gentle savior.
Give us nightly renewal
so we can better serve the gods.

Dream

Long-winged Morpheus,
messenger of future events,
supreme prophet to mortals,
in the sweet silence of sleep
you arrive without a sound,
speaking to the soul.
Exciting our minds
in our slumber, you whisper
the will of the immortals.

In every way bring us closer
to our destined path.
Reveal the concealed
signatures of fate.
Let no deceitful apparitions
show us signs of ill omen.
We beg you, holy one,
show us the will of the gods.

Death

You reward all
with a somber wreath
of asphodel and parsley,
the flower and the herb
of the cemetery.

You direct the path of mortals.
Your absence gives
the sacred gift of time.

With your perpetual sleep
you break the hold
of bodies on souls.

Undoing earth's strong bonds
you take from us all
what we hold most precious.

Deaf to begging and pleading
you execute Necessity's verdict,
which no one escapes.

We honor you.
Lead us away from
the wheel of deep grief
to the meadow of truth.

Liberator of the ripened soul, ·
revealer of our secrets,
inspire us to love life.

Annotated Bibliography

As the reader can see by glancing over this bibliography, we are living during a renaissance in Orphic studies. Search the titles online if you would like to learn more. Many of these works, or excerpts from them, can be read for free. Please consider this a suggested reading list. It includes highly technical works and historically significant studies, as well as works for beginners. Though comprehensive, this bibliography is not limited to academic studies. For more comprehensive bibliographies, please see Alberto Bernabé's "Orphic Bibliography" in *Tracing Orpheus* (edited by Miguel Herrero de Jáuregui et al.) and "Compiled Bibliography" in *The "Orphic" Gold Tablets and Greek Religion: Further Along the Path* (edited by Radcliffe G. Edmonds): both books are listed in this bibliography.

Addy, Crystal. 2012. "Oracles of Orpheus? The Orphic Gold Tablets" in *The International Journal of the Platonic Tradition 6*. Leiden: Brill.

Agnew, Vanessa. 2008. *Enlightenment Orpheus: The Power of Music in Other World*. Oxford: Oxford University Press.
> In a world where Captain Cook's travels to faraway places produced wonders that included transcriptions of Polynesian music, Orpheus who sailed on the *Argo* became a popular figure. A fascinating study of the influence of the Neoplatonist interpretation of Orpheus and the Orphic mysteries among composers during the Enlightenment in this history of a key moment in the evolution of German music.

Alderink, Larry J. 1981. *Creation and Salvation in Ancient Orphism*. Chico, Calif.: Scholar's Press.
> Indispensable comprehensive study of the central Orphic myths. Detailed criticism of earlier studies. Translation and discussion of the important Derveni papyrus, discovered in 1962 in Northern Greece, one of the earliest

Orphic artifacts (fourth century BCE). "It was found in one of four graves with a buried warrior's equipment, a spear and a javelin; a nearby tomb contained a krater portraying Dionysus surrounded by naked satyrs and maenads, wooing Ariadne." An education in critical scholarship, method, and objectivity. Includes important translations of Walter Burkert; valuable quotes from H. J. Rose, like this about the evidence for organized Orphic religion: "In somewhat the same manner there has never been a church called Puritan yet 'Puritan' and 'Puritanism' meant something in the religious history of Great Britain and the U.S.A." Lucid analysis of Pindar. Hermeneutics, Ludwig Wittgenstein, and Venn diagrams expertly used to clarify. Alderink mentions a Jewish Orphism between second century BCE and second century CE. He argues that the Orphics did not believe in transmigration but did believe souls preexist and survive bodies. But Arthur Evans in *The God of Ecstasy* points out: "The notion of Larry Alderink that Orphism is merely 'a mood or a spirit which animates selected literary texts' is refuted by Plato, who explicitly says in *The Republic* (364E) that the Orphics had books and ritual practices" (1988, 158).

Afonasina, Anna. 2007. "Shamanism and the Orphic tradition." Available online at Academia.edu.

Allen, M. J. B. 1995. "Summoning Plotinus: Ficino, Smoke and the Strangled Chickens." In *Plato's Third Eye: Studies in Marsilio Ficino's Metaphysics and Its Sources*. Abingdon, Oxfordshire, UK: Routledge.

Artemidorus. 2012. *Artemidorus' Oneirocritica: Text, Translation, and Commentary*. Translated with commentary by Daniel E. Harris-McCoy. Oxford: Oxford University Press.
 At long last a new translation with scholarly accoutrements. Interesting reflections on the Orphic mysteries and Dionysus in several of the dream interpretations.

Athanassakis, Apostolos N., and Benjamin Wolkow, trans. 2013. *The Orphic Hymns*. Baltimore, Md.: Johns Hopkins University Press.
 Includes the Greek text with an eloquent literal translation and copious notes.

Bachofen, J. J. 1967. *Myth, Religion, and Mother Right*. Translated by Ralph Manheim. Princeton, N.J.: Princeton University Press.
 Valuable discussions of Dionysus, Aphrodite, Demeter, and Apollo, with emphasis on the suppression of matriarchy. Bachofen, writing in 1861, introduced the word *matriarchy*.

Balfiore, Peter Joseph, tr. 2007. "Rainer Maria Rilke: Orpheus, Eurydice, Hermes" in *Literary Imagination*, Volume 9, Issue 3 (2007): 351–53.

Bamford, Christopher, ed. 1994. *Homage to Pythagoras: Rediscovering Sacred Science*. Hudson, N.Y.: Lindisfarne Books.

Bayard, Jean-Pierre. 2020. *Esoteric Mysteries of the Underworld: The Power and Meaning of Subterranean Sacred Spaces*. Translated by Jon E. Graham. Rochester, Vt.: Inner Traditions.
    An English translation of the classic work from 1961.

Bays, Gwendolyn. 1964. *The Orphic Vision: Seer Poets from Novalis to Rimbaud*. Lincoln: University of Nebraska.

Beatrice, Pier Franco. 2005. "On the Meaing of 'Profane' in the Pagan Christian Conflict of Late Antiquity: The Fathers, Firmicus Maternus and Prophyry before the Orphic 'Prorrheisis'" in *Illinois Classical Studies*, Vol. 30 (2005), 137–65, University of Illinois Press.

Bernabé, Alberto, and Ana Cristobal. 2008. *Instructions for the Netherworld: The Orphic Gold Tablets*. Boston: Brill.
    Exhaustively researched and lavishly illustrated with line drawings. Bernabé argues that denying the gold tablets are Orphic requires admitting the possibility of some other religion we know nothing about; therefore, it makes more sense to accept that they are indeed Orphic. With Radcliffe G. Edmonds representing the loyal opposition, Bernabé has advanced Orphic studies significantly.

Bernabé, Albertus. 1988. *Orphai Concordantia*. New York: Weidmann. Indispensable concordance to the Greek text.

Bernal, Martin. 1987. *Black Athene: The Afro-Asiatic Roots of Classical Civilization*. New Brunswick, N.J.: Rutgers University Press.
    Monumental study of the "fabrication of Greece" by European scholars from the eighteenth to the twentieth century. Bernal argues against the Aryan bias that sees classical Greek civilization as an evolution of the culture of the Indo-Aryan invaders. Bernal reminds us that ancient Greek sources credit ancient Egypt and Phoenicia as the roots of classical civilization. In the prehistoric period of Greek history, Egypt at the height of its power may have colonized Greece; Athens, the city of Athena, may have begun as an Egyptian colony named after the Egyptian goddess Neith. The Phoenicians had a colony on the Greek island Thera.

Bernstock, Judith. 1991. *Under the Spell of Orpheus: The Persistence of a Myth in Twentieth-Century Art*. Carbondale, Ill.: Southern Illinois University Press.

Betegh, Gabor. 2007. *The Derveni Papyrus: Cosmology, Theology and Interpretation*. Cambridge, UK: Cambridge University Press.
    Definitive analysis with useful indexes and an excellent bibliography.

Blanchot, Maurice. 1981. *The Gaze of Orpheus and Other Literary Essays.* Barrytown, N.Y.: Station Hill Press.

Blavatsky, H. P. 1877. *Theology.* Vol. 2 of *Isis Unveiled: A Master Key to the Mysteries of Ancient and Modern Science and Technology.* New York: J. W. Bouton.

Bohme, Robert. 1991. *Der Lykomide: Tradition und Wandel zwischen Orpheus und Homer.* Bern, Germany: Paul Haupt.

Borgeaud, Phillippe. 1988. *The Cult of Pan in Ancient Greece.* Translated by Kathleen Atlass and James Redfield. Chicago: University of Chicago Press.
  Study of the Pan cult with detailed attention to festivals and Pan's associations with Artemis, Hecate, nymphs, and satyrs. Discussion of nympholepsy, a condition suffered by ancient Greeks from Athenian teenagers to mighty Socrates himself, whereby a person in the woods would suddenly be overcome by intense elation. This was considered possession by a nymph. Some would run away into the woods never to return.

————. 1991. *Orphisme et Orphee: en l'honneur de Jean Rudhardt.* Paris: Librairie Droz.

Bremmer, Jan N. 1983. *The Early Greek Concept of the Soul.* Princeton, N.J.: Princeton University Press.
  To the ancient Greeks to live meant to ensoul. Bremmer's brief but comprehensive and definitive study suggests a widespread belief that human beings have two souls. The soul that is the life of the body is not the same as the free soul, which is known only in dreams and the afterlife.

————. 2002. *The Rise and Fall of the Afterlife.* London: Routledge.
  A summary of then current scholarship on the Orphic mysteries is included in this fascinating study of the evolution of the afterlife in the Western imagination, from the Orphic meadow in the world of the dead to modern near-death experiences. Along the way, Bremmer explores the origin of the idea of paradise and answers the question, Why did the followers of Jesus call themselves Christians? Bremmer concludes with these wry words: "What do the modern NDEs tell us about the afterlife? In opposition to what has often been suggested, they do not seem to prove the existence of the 'life everlasting' but testify to the continuing decline of the afterlife. Heaven is still made of gold and marble, but it is rather empty, except for a few relatives—evidently, every age gets the afterlife it deserves" (102).

————. 2016. "Shamanism in Classical Scholarship: Where Are We Now?" in *Horizons of Shamanism: a Triangular Approach to the History and Anthropology* of Ecstatic Techniques. Edited by Peter Jackson, 52–78. Stockholm: Stockholm University Press.

Breslin, Joesph. n.d. A Greek Prayer. Malibu, Calif.: J. Paul Getty Museum. Museum pamphlet.

Brisson, Luc. 2004. How Philosophers Saved Myths: Allegorical Interpretation and Classical Mythology. Chicago: University of Chicago Press.
    Exhaustive study of the use of allegory, with an excellent chapter on Pythagoreanism and Platonism. Detailed consideration of the allegorical approach of the Neoplatonists, including Proclus and Syrianus. These allegories inspired philosophers and artists long after the triumph of Christianity.

Brown, Robert. 1877. The Great Dionysiak Myth. London: Longmans, Green.
    Comprehensive but dated compilation of references and theories regarding Dionysus. As the author writes: "With respect to my chief modern authorities, and in order to satisfy the reader at the outset that the views of various important writers have not been overlooked, I have consulted the leading Assyriologists and Egyptologists of the time" (vi).

Burkert, Walter. 1972. Lore and Science in Ancient Pythagoreanism. Translated by Edwin L. Minar Jr. Cambridge, Mass.: Harvard University Press.
    As Jonathan Barnes wrote in The Presocratic Philosophers, Burkert with this book advanced to a new level of sanity and scholarship in the study of Pythagoreanism. Filled with fascinating information about Platonic metaphysics. Includes analysis of reincarnation in Orphism and Pythagoreanism, comparing and contrasting metempsychosis with shamanism.

———. 1981. "Craft versus Sect: The Problem of Orphics and Pythagoreans." In Self-Definition in the Graeco-Roman World, 1–22. Vol. 3 of Jewish and Christian Self-Definition, edited by Ben F. Meyer and E. P. Sanders. Philadelphia: Fortress Press.

———. 1989. Ancient Mystery Cults. Cambridge, Mass.: Harvard University Press.
    Important but controversial study. Burkert views the various mysteries as something like expensive clubs for the elite offering experiences related to reassurance about the afterlife, among other things. He supposes that Christianity because of its appeal to ordinary people and emphasis on family became more popular.

———. 1998. The Orientalizing Revolution: Near Eastern Influence on Greek Culture in the Early Archaic Age. Translated by Margaret E. Pinder. Cambridge, Mass.: Harvard University Press.
    Soothsayers, craftsmen, and poets from the Near East influenced ancient

247

Greek culture. Includes consideration of the sort of itinerant Orphic that the Derveni papyrus called "he who makes the sacred his craft," a sacred technician.

Butler, E. M. 1948. *Myth of the Magus.* New York: Macmillan.

Butterworth, E. A. S. 1970. *The Tree at the Navel of the Earth.* Berlin: De Gruyter.
Butterworth's theory that Homer's *Odyssey* records the hostile reaction of traditional Greek culture to an incursion from the East provides an interesting perspective. The lotus eaters are yogis with their talk of the jewel in the lotus, and the single eye of the Cyclops is a humorous exaggeration of the third eye of Hindu deities. The Orphic mysteries of purification to achieve full awareness in the afterlife are similar to yogic and tantric practices.

Campbell, Joseph. 1962. *Oriental Mythology.* Vol. 2 of *The Masks of God.* New York: Viking.

————. 1964. *Occidental Mythology.* Vol. 3 of *The Masks of God.* New York: Viking.
A few important words about the origins of Orphism and its similarities to Hindu Shiva worship.

————. 1974. *The Mythic Image.* Princeton, N.J.: Princeton University Press.
The world as dream and other themes of yoga traced through worldwide mutations and parallels from the Australian Bushmen to the ancient civilizations of Greece, China, and Africa. Beautifully illustrated.

Casadiegos, Yidy Páez. 2012. "Orpheus or the Soteriological Reform of the Dionysian Mysteries" in *American Journal of Sociological Research* 2012, 2(3): 38–51.

Cheak, Aaron. 2004. "Magic through the Linguistic Lenses of Greek mágos, Indo-European *mag(h)-, Sanskrit mâyâ and Pharaonic Egyptian heka." Ph.D. Dissertation: University of Queensland.

Chrysanthou, Anthi. 2020. *Defining Orphism: The Beliefs, the Teletae and the Writings. Trends in Classics: Supplementary Volumes,* vol. 94. Berlin: De Gruyter.

Cook, Arthur Bernard. 1914–1940. *Zeus: A Study in Ancient Religion.* 3 vols. Cambridge, UK: Cambridge University Press.
The classic study of the Zeus cult, distinguished by extensive, exhaustive scholarship, deserves the attention of any student of ancient Greek religion and culture. The index is a comprehensive collection of the attributes and myths of the Greek gods and goddesses. Available free at Internet Archive.

Cooper, Barry. 2001. "'A Lump Bred Up in Darknesse': Two Tellurian Themes of the Republic." In *Politics, Philosophy, Writing: Plato's Art of Caring for Souls,* edited by Zdravko Planinc, 80–121. Columbia: University of Missouri Press.

"The core of Orphism was the experience of ritual purification, a private mystery that involved the initiate in a renewal of life. It contained no service to a god but was a participatory transformation and the beginning of a new stage of life or a new public era. A central teaching, which Plato used from time to time, was that the body, soma, was a tomb, sema (see Crat. 400C; Gorg. 493a). This was implicit in the story of Orphic Dionysus from which was drawn the belief that deliverance from the body-tomb could only come through purity, which in turn could not be attained without initiation, followed by adherence to the Orphic life, which included moral goodness" (101). Cooper cites W. K. C. Guthrie and F. M. Cornford to support his position and dismisses E. R. Dodds as "grumpy."

Copenhaver, Brian P. (2022). *Life of Giovanni Pico della Mirandola. Oration.* Boston, Mass.: Harvard University Press.

Cornford, F. M. 1903. "Plato and Orpheus." *Classical Review* 17 (9): 433–45.
Dated but useful, thoughtful analysis of Plato's Cave, Euripides, and Pindar. Cornford quotes the *Phaedrus* to illustrate the Orphic theme in Platonism: "Soul universally cares for the soulless and ranges throughout all heaven passing into various forms. So, when it is perfect and winged, it voyages aloft and governs the whole Kosmos; but the soul which loses its wings falls till it meets with some solid thing which it takes for a dwelling."

Crisos, Tony. 2021. *The Orphic Tradition and the Rosicrucian Manifestos.* The Chancellor Robert R Livingston Masonic Library lecture, March 2018.

Crowley, Aleister. 1905. *Orpheus: A Lyrical Legend.* 4 vols. Inverness, Scotland: Society for the Propagation of Religious Truth.

Culianu, Ioan P. 1987. *Eros and Magic in the Renaissance.* Chicago: University of Chicago Press.

Danielou, Alain. 1992. *Gods of Love and Ecstasy: The Traditions of Shiva and Dionysus.* Rochester Vt.: Inner Traditions.
Startling apocalyptic mysticism and revelations of similarities in Greek and Hindu religion by a devoted student of both. Danielou, author of the classic *Hindu Polytheism* (Princeton, N.J.: Princeton University Press, 1964), was a great musician, artist, and athlete and one of the first Anglo-Saxons enrolled as a Hindu in the central shrine of Hinduism. He defended the Hindu caste system, and himself, against charges of racism.

D'Aoust, Jason R. 2013. "The Orpheus Figure: The Voice in Writing, Music and Media." Ph.D. diss., University of Western Ontario.

de Gébelin, Antoine Court. 1773–1782. *Le Monde Primitif.* Paris: Chez l'auteur.

Detienne, Marcel. 1977. *Dionysus Slain*. Translated by Mireille and Leonard Muellner. Baltimore, Md.: Johns Hopkins University Press.
> Penetrating discussion of the Dionysian myth of sacrifice with a long chapter on Orphism and Orphic prohibitions against animal sacrifice and meat eating. Albert Henrichs argues that Detienne confuses myth and cult (1984, 205–40). For criticism of Henrich's position see Arthur Evans (1988, 156).

———. 1989. "Culinary Practices and the Spirit of Sacrifice." In *The Cuisine of Sacrifice*, edited by Marcel Detienne and Jean-Pierre Vernant, translated by Paula Wissing, 1–20. Chicago: University of Chicago Press.
> Witty, sane essay reminding us most ancient Greek participants in sacrifice ate the animals they slaughtered during community feasts; the gods and goddesses feasted on smoke because immortals couldn't hunger for corruptible and therefore corrupted food.

———. 2003. *The Writings of Orpheus: Greek Myth in Cultural Context*. Translated by Janet Lloyd. Baltimore, Md.: Johns Hopkins University Press.
> Far more than a consideration of the Orphic tradition, this book shows how myths evolve and continue to inform generations of philosophical and cultural development. He leaves us to ponder the mystery of a hero despised by women: "It is even said that the excessive audacity" of the murderesses of Orpheus "stemmed from wine and on that day forward their men folk never went into battle sober. The Orphic tradition, which is consistently misogynous, suggests that Orpheus's singing could triumph over anything, attracting to it even stones and forest animals, subjugating Satyrs and Sirens, and winning over the frenzied Thracian warriors. It could triumph over anything except the female species, before which it was powerless. The voice of Orpheus failed when he faced the race of women, and they treated him the way the Titans treated infant Dionysus" (163–64).

Dickie, Matthew. 2003. *Magic and Magicians in the Greco-Roman World*. London: Routledge.
> Sorcerers, wandering miracle makers and conjurors, and their clients, including prostitutes, chariot drivers, and actors, provide a view of the shadow world of Greco-Roman culture where Orpheus became a byword for spell peddlers and the Orphic mysteries were mimicked by private groups as a social novelty.

Dio Chrysostom. 1951. *Dio Chrysostom with an English translation by J. W. Cohoon*. Harvard University Press.

Dodds, E. R. 1964. *The Greeks and the Irrational*. Cambridge, UK: Cambridge University Press.

Dodds discusses the differences between Orpheus and Orphism, reminding us that even primary Orphic materials such as the gold plates, Aristophanes's *The Birds*, and the myths of Plato may not be Orphic. He finds no evidence to believe that *soma sema* is Orphic. Dodds proposes Scythian or Thracian shamanism as the origin of Orphic myth. Careful of Ivan Linforth's analytical rigor, Dodds concludes Orpheus was a "mythical shaman or prototype of shamans." For a summary of Dodds, see Alderink (1981, 14) and McGinty (1978, 181).

d'Olivet, Fabre. 1995. *The Golden Verses of Pythagoras*. Translated by Nayán Louise Redfield. Cutchogue, N.Y.: Solar Press. First published 1813.

———. 2007. *Hermeneutic Interpretation of the Origin of the Social State of Man and of the Destiny of the Adamic Race*. Translated by Nayán Louise Redfield. San Rafael, Calif.: Hermetica. First published 1915.

Dreitlein, Thomas Eijō. 2011. "An Annotated Translation of Kūkai's Secret Key to the Heart Sūtra" in *Kōyasan Daigaku Mikkyō Bunka Kenkyūsho Kiyō* (高野山大学密教文化研究所紀要, The Bulletin of the Research Institute of Esoteric Buddhist Culture, Kōyasan University), Vol. 24, Feb. 2011, pp. 216–170 (reverse numbered).

Dunn, Patrick. 2018. *The Orphic Hymns: A New Translation for the Occult Practitioner*. Woodbury, Minn.: Llewellyn.
    Excellent scholarship with a wealth of notes. Includes the original Greek text. Indispensable for occultists with Orphic interests.

Eisler, Robert. 1921. *Orpheus the Fisher. Comparative Studies in Orphic and Early Christian Cult Symbolism*. London: J.M. Watkins.

Edmonds, Radcliffe G. III. 1999. "Tearing Apart the Zagreus Myth: A Few Disparaging Remarks on Orphism and Original Sin." *Classical Antiquity Journal* 18 (1): 35–73.
    Edmonds reveals the unfortunate habit of historians projecting their own beliefs and context onto their subjects. Believers in original sin convinced themselves that the Orphic myths foreshadowed Christianity not just in the murder of the savior Orpheus, but also in the myth of the Titans tearing apart baby Dionysus, thereby tainting all human beings with spiritual impurity.

———. 2004. *Myths of the Underworld Journey: Plato, Aristophanes, and the "Orphic" Gold Tablets*. Cambridge, UK: Cambridge University Press.
    The quotation marks around the word *Orphic* in Edmonds's work perhaps best summarizes his position, but his rigorous scholarship makes his work exemplary

of the prevailing agnostic stance toward the idea of any unified Orphic religious movement. "Is Orphism an origin or an orientation?" he asks. With Alberto Bernabé representing the loyal opposition, Edmonds leads the way among the new generation of Orphic scholars.

———. 2006. "To Sit in Solemn Silence? Thronosis in Ritual, Myth and Iconography." *American Journal of Philology* 127 (3): 347–66.
Fascinating study of the ritual of "solemn silence" in the Eleusinian mysteries, a meditation, probably on mortality, as the aspiring initiate would be draped in a death shroud. Some reflections on the Orphic mysteries, which may have involved a similar procedure. Jane Harrison believed aspirants entered through a cave painted with the terrors of human life including war, disease, decrepitude, and death.

———. 2008. "Extra-Ordinary People: Mystai and Magoi, Magicians and Orphics in the Derveni Papyrus." *Classical Philology* 103: 16–39.
Edmonds reveals how the author of the papyrus viewed himself as different from his colleagues or competitors, to a certain degree illuminating the difference between the approaches to ritual that became in the English language the mystic and the ceremonial magician. A must-read, available online thanks to Classics Common.

———. 2008. "Recycling Laertes' Shroud: More on Orphism and Original Sin." Center for Hellenic Studies. Cambridge, Mass.: Harvard University Press.
It begins: "Alberto Bernabé has compared the scholarship on Orphism in the past century to the web of Penelope, a succession of cunning weavings of the threads followed by unravelings, in which any apparent progress in formulating a coherent picture of Orphism by one wave of scholars is undone by the next group of critics."

———. 2009. "A Curious Concoction: Tradition and Innovation in Olympiodorus' 'Orphic' Creation of Mankind." *American Journal of Philology* 130 (4): 511–32.

———. 2010. "The Children of Earth and Starry Heaven: The Meaning and Function of the Formula in the 'Orphic' Gold Tablets." In *Orfeo y el orfismo: Nuevas perspectivas,* edited by Alberto Bernabé, Francesc Casadesús, and Marco Antonio Santamaría, 98–121. Alicante, Spain: Biblioteca Virtual Miguel de Cervantes.
Careful analysis of what we know and don't know about the famous Orphic formula.

———, ed. 2011. *The "Orphic" Gold Tablets and Greek Religion: Further along the Path: Recent Studies in the Orphic Gold Leaves.* Cambridge, UK: Cambridge University Press.

Thirteen essays including facsimile texts and translations of gold tablets. In-depth analysis of context from multiple perspectives provides the latest scholarship. Edmonds in his own contribution wonders if we are dealing with sacred scriptures or oracles of the dead. Could the famous "I am a child of earth and starry heaven" have been originally understood as a report from the afterlife?

———. 2013. *Redefining Ancient Orphism: A Study in Greek Religion.* Cambridge, UK: Cambridge University Press.
The latest scholarship presented by a renowned expert whose writing skills make the adventure that much more enjoyable.

Eggyed, Attila. 2020. "A Syntactic Approach to the Orphic Gold Leaves" in *Archive für Religionsgeschicht* Volume 21–22, Issue 1.

Encyclopedia Britannica. 1948. S.v. "Aphrodite," "Apollo," "Ares," "Artemis," "Athena," "Dionysus," "Greek Religion," "Hecate," "Hephaestus," "Hera," "Hercules," "Hermes," "Orpheus," "Poseidon," "Thyrsus," "Zeus."
Dated but informative summaries attentive to details of cult.

Evans, Arthur. 1988. *The God of Ecstasy: Sex-Roles and the Madness of Dionysos.* New York: St. Martin's Press.
Study of Dionysus focusing on the *Bacchae* of Euripides. Includes an excellent translation of the *Bacchae* and a wealth of interesting quotations from the *Dionysica of Nonnos* and from Plutarch: "Plutarch mentions that Philip and Olympias, the parents of Alexander the Conqueror, first met when they were both initiated into an Orphic cult in Samothrace in the North" (157). Evans surveys the myth of Dionysus from its origins to its modern variations. Along the way he analyzes Athenian law, ancient Greek attitudes toward homosexuality, and the plight of women in ancient Greece: in democratic Athens rape was usually considered the victim's fault, the law compelled husbands to divorce raped wives, and punishment for rape was "only a fine." Chapters on Rome and India (including an essential criticism of Alain Danielou's work) and a chapter on Dionysus and Christ with comments on the witch persecution. Evans also summarizes and critiques Albert Henrich's important articles on Dionysus and Orphism.

Faraone, Christopher A. 2011. "Rushing into Milk: New Perspectives on the Gold Tablets." Chapter 13 in *The "Orphic" Gold Tablets and Greek Religion: Further Along the Path,* edited by Radcliffe G. Edmonds III, 304–24. Cambridge, UK: Cambridge University Press.

Farnell, Lewis R. 1896. *The Cults of the Greek States.* Oxford: Oxford University Press.
The classic collection on ancient Greek religion. Exhaustive but dated.

Ferrari, Franco. 2015. "Orphics at Olbia?" Academia.edu.

Fideler, David. 1993."Orpheus and the Mysteries of Harmony." *Gnosis: A Journal of the Western Inner Traditions* 27: 20–35.
>   The publisher of Phanes Press explores the magical power of music, the story of Orpheus, and the nature of musical harmony in ancient cosmological symbolism, both pagan and Christian.

Field, Arthur M. 2014. *The Origins of the Platonic Academy of Florence.* Princeton, N.J.: Princeton University Press.

Fontenrose, Joseph. 1959. *Python.* Berkeley: University of California Press.
>   Interesting parallels to Orpheus in this classic work on the mythology of the Oracle of Delphi.

———. 1978. *The Delphic Oracle.* Berkeley: University of California Press, 1978.
>   Bits and pieces about Orpheus in the notes on this collection of questions and answers of the Oracle of Delphi.

Fowden, Garth. 1986. *The Egyptian Hermes: A Historical Approach to the Late Pagan Mind.* Princeton, N.J.: Princeton University Press.
>   Valuable examination of early Hermeticism and its relation and resemblance to the Greek Magical Papyri, gnostic holy books, and the theurgy of Iamblichus.

Freedman, Ralph. 1998. *Life of a Poet: Rainer Maria Rilke.* Evanston, Ill.: Northwestern University Press.

Freiert, William K. 1991. "Orpheus: A Fugue on the Polis." In *Myth and the Polis,* edited by Dora C. Pozzi and John M. Wickersham, 32–48. *Myth and Poetics* series, edited by Gregory Nagy. Ithaca, N.Y.: Cornell University Press.
>   Includes an interesting consideration of Orpheus from the shamanistic implications of his journey to the underworld to rescue Eurydice to the meaningful overtones of Cocteau's Orphic creations. Freiert reminds us: "The myth of Orpheus appears as nonheroic, alien to the warrior-hunter ethic, and alien to the poetry of praise (*kleos*) and blame that legitimizes heroic behavior in the archaic Greek society" (38).

Friedman, John Block. 1970. *Orpheus in the Middle Ages.* Cambridge, Mass.: Harvard University Press.
>   Important study of medieval mutations of Orphic myth including the fable that Moses taught Orpheus in Egypt, a look at the use of Orphic themes in representations of Jesus Christ in the art of late antiquity, the evolving story of his lost love Eurydice, and the popular theme of King Orpheus and his queen. Students of Hermetic literature will find much useful information. Don't be dissuaded by the occasional chunk of untranslated Latin.

Fritz, Kurt Von. 1940. *Pythagorean Politics in Southern Italy: An Analysis of the Sources.* New York: Columbia University Press.

    This examination of Aristoxenos and Dikaiarchos, and their sources, weighs their reliability and then "reconstructs" the Pythagorean information in Plato's Timaeus. Questions of chronology and consideration of evidence from coins receives attention, as does the character of Pythagorean politics, including an illuminating comparison with the political history of Freemasonry pointing out that the leaders of both were probably immune from the persecutions others of their orders suffered. Fritz, a Prussian, was forced to retire from teaching in Germany because he would not take the oath to Hitler. He taught at Oxford, at Reed College in Portland, and, after 1937, at Columbia University.

Garland, Robert. 1985. *The Greek Way of Death.* Ithaca, N.Y.: Cornell University Press.

    Meticulous survey of ancient Greek funeral customs, mythology, and folklore.

Gayton, A. H. 1935. "The Orpheus Myth in North America" in *The Journal of American Folklore,* Vol. 48, no. 189 (July–September).

Gesner, Matthias. 1764. *Orphei Argonautica Libellus de Lapidibus et Fragmenta.* Leipzig, Germany: Sumbtibus Caspari Fritsch.

    This pioneering German scholar gathered together all materials available at the time related to Orpheus including hymns, the *Orphic Argonautica,* and fragments from around the time that the Hanging Gardens of Babylon were established.

Gill, Carolyn Bailey, ed. (1996) *Maurice Blanchot: The Demand of Writing.* New York, NY: Routledge.

Gilly, Carlos, and Sebastiano Gentile. 1999. *Marsilio Ficino e il ritorno di Ermete Trismegisto.* Amsterdam, Netherlands: Bibliotheca Philosophica Hermetica.

Godwin, Joscelyn. 1984. "The Golden Chain of Orpheus: A Survey of Musical Esotericism in the West." *Temenos* 4: 7–25; *Temenos* 5: 211–39.

    Important and delightful, with Godwin's impeccable scholarship.

———. 1994. *The Theosophical Enlightenment.* Albany: State University of New York Press.

———. 2005. *The Pagan Dream of the Renaissance.* Newburyport, Mass.: Red Wheel.

———. 2014. *The Golden Thread: The Ageless Wisdom of the Western Mystery Traditions.* Wheaton, Il.: Quest Books.

Goodrick-Clarke, Nicholas. (2008). *The Western Esoteric Traditions: A Historical Introduction*. USA: Oxford University Press.

Graf, Fritz, and Sarah Iles Johnston. 2007. *Ritual Texts for the Afterlife: Orpheus and the Bacchic Gold Tablets*. London: Routledge.
> Students of Walter Burkert continue his fine tradition of scholarship, providing new information about the enigmatic gold tablets, including a translation and survey of previous scholarship.

Graves, Robert. 1948. *The White Goddess: A Historical Grammar of Poetic Myth*. London: Faber and Faber.
> Graves's controversial study of tree alphabets and the origins of the muse myth occasionally sheds an interesting light on Orphism: "A famous Greek picture by Polygnotus at Delphi represented Orpheus as receiving the gift of mystic eloquence by touching willow-trees in a grove of Persephone" (174). According to Graves in the theology brought by Orphics to Rome, Hera is "physical nature," Zeus is the "impregnating or animating principle" symbolized by the sun, and Athena is the "directing wisdom behind the universe," symbolized by the moon, perhaps because observing the moon's phases and tides taught human beings to measure.

———. 1957. *The Greek Myths*. 2 vols. New York: Braziller.
> Wonderful handbook collection of the complete Greek myths supported by footnotes mostly related to *The White Goddess*.

Griffin, Michael. 2012. "Proclus on Place as the Luminous Vehicle of the Soul." *Dionysius* 30: 161–86.

Guthrie, Kenneth Sylvan, trans. 1988. *The Pythagorean Sourcebook and Library: An Anthology of Ancient Writings Which Relate to Pythagoras and Pythagorean Philosophy*. Edited and with an introduction by David R. Fideler. Grand Rapids, Mich.: Phanes Press.
> Reprint of Guthrie's obscure classic with many valuable additions.

Guthrie, W. K. C. 1951. "The Orphics." Chapter 11 in *The Greeks and Their Gods*, 307–31. Boston: Beacon Press.
> A brief but informative chapter on Orphism. Among other interesting points, Guthrie reminds us that Empedokles, the "philosopher, scientist, poet, orator, statesman, mystagogue, miracle worker, healer, and claimant to divine honors," as the *Oxford Classical Dictionary* put it, was a passionate believer in Orphism. For a summary and criticism of Guthrie, see McGinty (1978, 188).

———. 1993. *Orpheus and Greek Religion*. Princeton, N.J.: Princeton University Press. First published 1952.

The bedrock study of Orphism. A wealth of essential translations including numerous quotes from Proclus. Clear and complete translation and discussion of Plato on Orpheus and reincarnation. "To us the differences between the worship of Olympian Zeus and the Mysteries of Demeter may seem as great as those between any two religions of modern times. Yet not only did they never lead to wars or persecutions, but it was perfectly possible for the same man to be a devout participant in both" (7). Excellent bibliography. For a summary of Guthrie, see Alderink (1981, 11–12) and McGinty (1978, 187). Unfortunately, McGinty does not discuss *Orpheus and Greek Religion* in depth.

Haddo, Oliver. 1909. "The Psychology of Hashish" *Equinox: The Review of Scientific Illuminism* 1 (2).

Harris, R. Baine, ed. 1982. *Neoplatonism and Indian Thought*. Albany, N.Y.: State University of New York Press.

Harrison, Jane. 1903. *Prolegomena to the Study of Greek Religion*. Cambridge, UK: Cambridge University Press.
According to Park McGinty, Harrison's book is "dated," and he notes that "tendentious pronouncements, programmatic generalizations, heartfelt exhortations, and autobiographical claims and confessions dot her work" (1978, 73, 75). Also according to McGinty, Harrison believed the Dionysian rites were "the product of mental backwardness" (1978, 21, 69, 71ff, 105, 221). Harrison was heavily influenced by the technique and perspective of Sir James George Frazier's *The Golden Bough*. She argues that the Orphic rites preserved the tribal memory of the original shaman dances. The maenads, satyrs, and koretes were mythic distortions of warriors dancing around bonfires. Harrison argues the Orphic mysteries originated in Crete.

————. 1912. *Themis: A Study of the Social Origins of Greek Religion*. Cambridge, UK: Cambridge University Press.
Harrison examines how local cult ancestor spirits evolved into Olympian gods. She analyzes a *Hymn to the Kouretes* for evidence of primitive rites. Nilsson dismissed this as "telescoping the millennia" (quoted in McGinty 1978, 223, n31). The latter half of the book is a discussion of Dike and Themis, that is Moral Right and Natural Law, heavily influenced by the "sociological evolutionism of Emile Durkheim and Bergson," according to McGinty (1978, 85, 86). McGinty quotes the British classicist G. S. Kirk, who wrote that Harrison is "lively, learned, yet unpedantic—and utterly uncontrolled by anything resembling careful logic" (1978, 210).

————. 1921. *Epilogomena to the Study of Greek Religion*. Cambridge, UK: Cambridge University Press.

> This work reflects the influence of Freudianism. As McGinty shows in *Interpretation and Dionysos,* Harrison suffered from a then prevalent belief in the stupidity of primitive man, yet she provides interesting insights into the similarities between shamanism and the myths of dancing warriors protecting baby Dionysus with their din.

Hartmann, Franz. 1896. *The Life of Philippus Theophrastus Bombast of Hohenheim, Known by the Name of Paracelsus and the Substance of His Teachings*. London: Kegan Paul, Trench, Trübner.

Hasty, Olga Peters. 1996. *Tsvetaeva's Orphic Journeys in the Worlds of the Word*. Evanston, Ill.: Northwestern University Press.

Heninger, S. K. Jr. 1974. *Touches of Sweet Harmony: Pythagorean Cosmology and Renaissance Poetics*. San Marino, Calif.: Angelico Press.

> A beautifully written and illustrated study of the influence of Orphism and Pythagoreanism on Shakespeare, Spenser, and the Elizabethans.

Henrichs, Albert. 1977. "Response." In *Orphism and Bacchic Mysteries: New Evidence and Old Problems of Interpretation; Protocol of the 28th Colloquy*, edited by Hermeneutical Studies in Hellenistic and Modern Culture, Walter Burkert, and Wilhelm H. Wuellner, 210–11. Berkeley, Calif.: Center for Hermeneutical Studies.

> Henrichs follows Linforth, doubting the evidence for organized Orphism. Arthur Evans uses philology to critique Henrichs; see Evans 1988, 156.

————. 1984. "Loss of Self, Suffering and Violence: The Modern View of Dionysus from Nietzsche to Girard." *Harvard Studies in Classical Philology* 88: 205–40.

Henry, Elisabeth. 1992. *Orpheus with His Lute: Poetry and the Renewal of Life*. Carbondale: Southern Illinois University Press.

> The philosophical and psychological mutations of Orpheus from catacomb iconography equating Orpheus with Jesus Christ to the medieval romances inspired by Ovid and the tragic love stories of Renaissance Orpheus

Herrero de Jáuregui, Miguel. 2010. *Orphism and Christianity in Late Antiquity*. Vol. 7 of *Sozomena: Studies in the Recovery of Ancient Texts,* edited by Alessandro Barchiesi, Robert Fowler, Dirk Obbink, and Nigel Wilson. Berlin: De Gruyter.

> Reveals how scholars "refabricated Orphism," finding in it projections of their own Protestant Christian beliefs. From dismissing Orphism as an invention of Neoplatonists desperately competing with Christianity to attacks on Catholic primacy based on Orphism as a precursor to Protestant Christianity,

the impact of unconscious prejudices and conscious agendas has warped our view of the Orphic mysteries.

————. 2011. *Tracing Orpheus: Studies of Orphic Fragments*. Edited by Miguel Herrero de Jáuregui, Ana Isabel Jiménez San Cristóbal, Marco Antonio Santamaria, and Eugenio R. Lujón. Vol. 10 of *Sozomena: Studies in the Recovery of Ancient Texts,* edited by Alessandro Barchiesi, Robert Fowler, Dirk Obbink, and Nigel Wilson. Berlin: De Gruyter.

Indispensable scholarship in the form of sixty-five short studies on Orphic fragments by leading experts; includes Bernabé's state-of-the-art Orphic bibliography.

————. 2015. "The Construction of Inner Religious Space in Wandering Religion of Classical Greece." *Numen: International Review for the History of Religions* 62 (5–6): 596–626.

————. 2016. "'Trust the God' *Tharsein* in Ancient Greek Religion." In *Harvard Studies in Classical Philology*, vol. 108. Edited by Richard F. Thomas. Boston: Harvard University Press.

Hibbert, Julian. 1828. *Plutarchus and Theophrastus on Superstition*. London: Privately published.

Irwin, Lee. 1991. "The Orphic Mystery: Harmony and Mediation." In *Alexandria 1,* edited by David Fideler, 37–55. Grand Rapids, Mich.: Phanes.

A concise and comprehensive summary and analysis in a journal with other excellent articles on ancient Greek music and religion.

Jaeger, Werner. 1948. *Paideia: The Ideals of Greek Culture*. New York: Oxford University Press.

Several interesting comments on Orphism in this thorough and thought pro-voking three-volume study of ancient Greek ideas about education.

Johnston, Sarah Iles. 1990. *Hekate Soteira: American Classical Studies 21*. Atlanta, Ga.: Scholar's Press.

In-depth look at the cult of Hekate from magic to theurgy, including her status as a Platonic cosmic soul.

————. 1999. *Restless Dead: Encounters between the Living and the Dead in Ancient Greece*. Berkeley: University of California.

This book concerns ghosts in ancient Greece and the rituals to honor them, thereby averting trouble: for example, female ghosts could cause "childless mothers and blighted virgins," and spirits who died by unavenged violence are problematic. The author explains how Hecate became the Mistress of

Ghosts and delineates the fine differences between the different beings most translators, including ourselves, have simply called the Furies. Orpheus and the Orphic mysteries are recurrent themes.

Jung, Carl G., M. L. Von Franz, Joseph L. Henderson, and Jolande Jacobi. 1968. *Man and His Symbols: A Popular Presentation of the Essential Ideas of Jungian Psychology.* New York: Doubleday.

Kastrup, Bernardo. 2016. *More Than Allegory: On Religious Myth, Truth And Belief.* Winchester, UK: Iff Books.

Katinis, Teodoro. 2010. "A Humanist Confronts the Plague: Ficino's Consilio Contro La Pestilentia." *Modern Language Notes* 125 (1): 72–83.

Kerenyi, Karl. 1959. *Asklepios.* Princeton, N.J.: Princeton University Press.
　　Comprehensive study of the god of healing. Kerenyi believes the Asclepius cult developed from shamanism. The ancient Greek depiction of Chiron the centaur reproduced in this book will remind tarot scholars of the fool card.

———. 1967. *Eleusis.* Princeton, N.J.: Princeton University Press.
　　Archaeological focus in a classical study of the Eleusinian mysteries. Many references to Orpheus and the Orphic hymns.

———. 1979. *The Gods of the Greeks.* London: Thames and Hudson.
　　Superior survey of Greek mythology; a scholarly handbook with constant attention to the details of epithets and cult.

———. 1983. *Apollo: The Wind, the Spirit, and the God; Four Studies.* Dallas, Tex.: Spring.
　　Detailed short study of Apollo revealing the importance of the wolf cult, often forgotten or glossed over.

Kern, Otto. 1920. *Eine Religionsgeschichtliche Untersuchung.* Berlin: Weidmann.
　　A brief but concentrated overview of the Orphic cult. Kern reports rumors that Orpheus was the grandfather or otherwise direct ancestor of Homer. Frontispiece photo of Kern—a stern, crewcut, long-bearded pioneering Orphic scholar from Bavaria.

———. 1922. *Orphicorum Fragmenta.* Berlin: Weidmann.
　　Meticulous and essential collection of texts.

Kingsley, Peter. 1995. *Ancient Philosophy, Mystery, and Magic: Empedocles and Pythagorean Tradition.* Cambridge, UK: Cambridge University Press.
　　Highly recommended masterpiece turned generations of scholarship on end by revealing the shamanistic implications of Empedocles and the usefulness

of Neoplatonic perspectives on the tradition they knew better than any modern scholar, having had access to lost books like Aristotle's work on Pythagoreanism and the entire Orphic corpus.

Klutstein, Ilana. 1987. *Marsilio Ficino et la théologie ancienne: Oracles chaldaïques, hymnes orphiques—hymnes de Proclus*. Florence, Italy: L.S. Olschki.

Kotansky, Roy. 2021. "Dialogues of the Dead on the 'Orphic' Gold Tablets" in David Saunders (ed.) *Underworld: Imagining the Afterlife in Ancient South Italian Vase Painting*. Los Angeles: J. Paul Getty Museum.

Kuznetsova, Anna S. 2007. "Shamanism and the Orphic Tradition." *Skepsis:* 24–31.
 Brief but illuminating look at the popular comparison between Orpheus and the shamans of certain indigenous cultures. Kuznetsova concludes: "Thus, an association of Orpheus with shamanism appears to be quite problematic in many respects. Those elements in the Orphica which are similar to certain typically shamanistic features remain unsupported in view of the other equally important criteria. Apollo and Dionysus, who occupied a distinctive place in the Greek mythology and were linked to specific religious cults, admit certain parallels with shamanistic rites, but I would warn against an easy connection of the other Greek religious practices with shamanism" (30).

Laks, André, and Glenn W. Most, eds. 1997. *Studies on the Derveni Papyrus*. Oxford: Oxford University Press.
 Important early collection of essays on the magical papyrus including its first English translation.

Lamberton, Robert. 1986. *Homer the Theologian: Neoplatonist Allegorical Reading and the Growth of the Epic Tradition*. Berkeley: University of California Press.
 Lamberton points out, following Burkert, that Platonism minus the Socratic dialectic, the dogma of the academy, may have been fundamentally neo-Pythagorean and that the Neoplatonic allegorical interpretation of Homer (and Orpheus) may go back much further in history than late antiquity. The chapter on Proclus highlights the symbolic subtleties of Homeric metaphor.

Lebedev, Andrei V. 2020. "The Theogony of Epimenides of Crete and the Origin of the Orphic-Pythagorean Doctrine of Reincarnation." Academia .edu. Originally published in Russian in 2015, *Proceedings of the Memorial Tronsky Conference*, 550–84.

———. 2022. "The Aegean origin and early history of the Greek doctrines of reincarnation and immortality of the soul: Epimenides, Pherecydes, Pythagoras, and Onomacritus' Orphica" in *Orientalia et Classica*. Moscow: Higher School of Economics, 2022.

A must read. Best introduction to Epimenides and Onomacritus.

Lévi, Éliphas. 1959. *The Key of the Mysteries*. London: Rider. First published 1861.

———. 2000. *The Great Secret or Occultism Unveiled*. York Beach, Me.: Samuel Weiser. First published 1868.

Liddell, Henry George, and Robert Scott. 1987. *Liddell and Scott's Greek-English Lexicon*. Oxford: Oxford University Press.
  Indispensable and holy to scholars of ancient Greek.

Linforth, Ivan M. 1941. *The Arts of Orpheus*. Berkeley: University of California Press.
  Focus on Orphic influence on Plato and the mainstream Attic culture. Devastating criticism of evidence for Orphism. Linforth argues Orphism never was a common creed or ceremony; it was "a category for those ancients interested in a vast miscellany of myth and religious lore." For a summary of Linforth see Alderink (1981, 10–11).

Lucid, Tamra. 2021. *Making the Ordinary Extraordinary: My Seven Years in Occult Los Angeles with Manly Palmer Hall*. Rochester, Vt.: Inner Traditions.
  Includes Lucid's account of the experience related in chapter 1 of this book.

Macchioro, Vittorio D. 1930. *From Orpheus to Paul: A History of Orphism*. New York: Henry Holt.
  "The summary consists partly of dogmatic assertions, partly of obvious mis-interpretations of Aristotle and Plutarch," writes Guthrie (1951, 246); but Macchioro presents a wealth of materials from which to draw one's own interpretation.

Macedo, José Marcos, Daniel Kölligan, and Pedro Barbieri. 2021. *Polyónymoi: A Lexicon of the Divine Epithets in the Orphic Hymns*. Würzburg, Germany: Würzburg University Press.

Mann, Jenny C. 2021. *The Trials of Orpheus: Poetry, Science, and the Early Modern Sublime*. Princeton, N.J.: Princeton University Press.

Martin, John Levi. 2017. "The Birth of the True, the Good, and the Beautiful: Toward an Investigation of the Structures of Social Thought: Reconstructing Social Theory, History and Practice Current Perspectives" in *Social Theory*, Volume 35.

Mastros, Sara L. 2022. *Orphic Hymns Grimoire*. West Yorkshire, UK: Hadean Press.
  Loyal to the text yet lyrical, with additional content to support ritual work.

McGahey, Robert. 1994. *The Orphic Moment: Shaman to Poet Thinker in Plato, Nietzsche, and Mallarmé*. Albany: State University of New York Press.

Reveals the deep influence of Orphic myth on philosophy and literature by examining Nietzsche and Mallarmé.

McGinty, Park. 1978. *Interpretation and Dionysos: Method in the Study of a God*. The Hague: Mouton.
An example of critical excellence, revealing the contexts and biases of the scholars constructing Orphic history. A wealth of quotations, such as Nietzsche on the intoxicating effect of Dionysus: "Now all the rigid, hostile barriers which need, caprice or 'insolent fashion' have fixed between men are smashed. Now, with the gospel of the world harmony, everyone feels not only united, reconciled, merged with his neighbor, but one with him, as though the veil of Maya had been torn and only fluttered in tatters before the mysterious primordial One" (40). Essential discussion of Walter F. Otto's important works on Dionysus. Excellent bibliography.

Mead, G. R. S. 1965. *Orpheus*. London: Watkins.
Good but dated scholarship from the author of *Thrice-Greatest Hermes*. Fold-out chart. An interesting overview.

Meisner, Dwayne. 2018. *Orphic Tradition and the Birth of the Gods*. Oxford: Oxford University Press.
Gathers and explores the Derveni, Eudemian, Hieronyman, and Rhapsodic or so-called Orphic creation myths.

Meyer, Marvin W., ed. 1987. *The Ancient Mysteries: A Sourcebook*. San Francisco: Harper and Row.
Modern translations and helpful notes; useful for studies of similarities and differences between the cults of the Euphrates and the Mediterranean.

Mishev, Georgi. 2012. *Thracian Magic: Past and Present*. London: Avolonia.

Morand, Anne-France. 2015. "The Narrative Techniques of the Orphic hymns" in *Hymnic Narrative and the Narratology of Greek Hymns, Mnemosyne Supplements, Mnemosyne Supplementa*. Boston: Brill, Leiden.

Moore, Thomas. 1990. *The Planets Within*. Great Barrington, Mass: Lindisfarne Press.
Detailed, seminal study of Ficino's fusion of Christian and classical theology and astrology and its influence on the Italian Renaissance. Ficino translated the Orphic hymns at the beginning of the Renaissance, performing them for his friends.

Moulinier, Louis. 1955. *Orphée et L'Orphisme à l'époque classique*. Paris: Les Belles Lettres.

Brief, but incisive. Moulinier follows Linforth, doubting the evidence. He summarizes the history of the argument that the slaughter of Dionysus by the Titans was not necessarily linked to the Titanic origin of humanity.

Nagy, Gregory. 2012. *Homer the Preclassic*. Berkeley: University of California Press.
The crowning achievement by the director of the Center for Hellenic Studies, the Francis Jones Professor of Classical Greek Literature, and professor of comparative literature at Harvard sheds interesting light on Orphism, including the question of Pythagoras writing poems under the name of Orpheus, as mentioned by Ion of Chios.

Newman, P. D. 2023. *Theurgy: Theory and Practice: The Mysteries of the Ascent to the Divine*. Rochester, Vt.: Inner Traditions.

Nilsson, M. P. 1935. "Early Orphism and Kindred Religious Movements." *Harvard Theological Review* 28: 181–230.
Nilsson argued that Dionysus is the "spirit of the fruit of the fields," based on the god's association with the *liknon,* a winnowing tool used for harvesting corn that was also used in the rites of Bacchus. But he later changed his mind, believing the evidence does not connect Dionysus to agriculture (see McGinty 1978, 228, n61).

———. 1971. *The Minoan-Mycenaean Religion and its Survival in Greek Religion*. New York: Biblo and Tannen.
For criticism and appreciation of Nilsson, see Guthrie (1951, 144); Alderink (1981, 13); and McGinty (1978). According to McGinty, Nilsson's work has "disturbing racist, sexist, elitist undertones" (1978, 123, 127, 229, n74, n83), and he notes that Nilsson argued that the Greeks viewed the incursion of the cult of Dionysus as an "atavistic regression" from Anatolia (122). Nevertheless, McGinty considered Nilsson's work the state of the art at that time (109).

Nixey, Catherine. 2017. *The Darkening Age: The Christian Destruction of the Classical World*. New York: Macmillan.
A must read for an understanding of the demise of the classical world.

Nock, Arthur Darby. 1972. "A Cult of Ordinance in Verse." In *Essays on Religion and the Ancient World,* vol. 2. Edited by Zeph Stewart. 415–21. Cambridge, Mass.: Harvard University Press.
Analysis of an inscription from a sanctuary of Dionysus in what is now Turkey. Nock elucidates the fine line between Pythagorean and Orphic. Nock wonders if Apollonius of Tyana or another wandering neo-Pythagorean may have established the ritual ordinance in question but concludes that the more likely scenario is that given the respect afforded to Orpheus and Pythagoras, their

prohibitions and ordinances were widely adopted. Nock points out that many of these prohibitions may have been mere quarantines for most participants who could not be expected to give up meat, beans, and sex except for prescribed periods. "Purity means thinking holy thoughts," he reminds us.

———. 1972. "Orphism or Popular Philosophy?" In *Essays on Religion and the Ancient World*, vol. 1. Edited by Zeph Stewart. 301–15. Cambridge, Mass.: Harvard University Press.
Dated but refreshingly skeptical viewpoint that challenged the fabricated Orphism of earlier scholars. Beliefs mistakenly classified as Orphic were popular in far wider circles, such as among the theosophists. Misinterpreted metaphors added to the confusion. Is the circle of necessity reincarnation or simply the falling leaves of autumn?

Ogden, Daniel. 2001. *Greek and Roman Necromancy*. Princeton, N.J.: Princeton University Press.
A chapter called "Shamans, Pythagoreans and Orphics" is included in this look at ancient Greek and Roman beliefs. Other chapters, covering various necromantic practices, are: "Tombs and Battlefields," "Oracles of the Dead," "Dream Incubation," and "Evocators, Sorcerors, and Ventriloquists."

Osek, Ewa. 2015. "The Orphic Diet." *Littera Antiqua* 10: 25–200.
Excellent and comprehensive consideration of Orphic vegetarianism and its relation to the similar Pythagorean dietary restriction, though not all Pythagoreans were vegetarian. Exploration of the example of Empedocles. Osek points out that these culinary guidelines were followed during the initiations in the mysteries of Eleusis and those of Demeter, but the Orphics made these taboos a lifelong practice.

Oxford Classical Dictionary. 1961. Oxford: Oxford University Press.
Not as comprehensive a collection of ancient sources as *Dr. Smith's Classical Dictionary* but essential.

Paget, R. F. 1967. *In Search of Orpheus*. New York: Roy.
Rogue scholar finds river Styx and possible site of Orphic mysteries. Well-translated generous collection of quotes about Orphism and quick introductions to myth and cult by the Indiana Jones of Orphic studies. Alderink writes: "out of touch or interest with the historical and scholarly problems" (1981, 99).

Parke, H. W. 1967. *The Oracles of Zeus: Dodona, Olympia, Ammon*. Cambridge, Mass.: Harvard University Press.
Parke reminds us that Dodona was a single tree not a grove. He believes the dove in the tree of Zeus was the ring dove, less common in Greece.

Parker, Robert. 1996. *Miasma: Pollution and Purification in Early Greek Religion*. Oxford: Oxford University Press.

> Essential study with many interesting perspectives on the Orphic mysteries. "An allusion in the Hippolytus shows that the link of Bacchic dances, Orphic books, and vegetarianism was familiar in fifth-century Athens. It is none the less plausible that purifiers did exist who would offer their clients salvation for the cost of a ritual, without insisting on the uncomfortable requirements of an Orphic life. It is interesting that Plato speaks of release, not from metempsychosis or Titanic guilt, but from the crimes of an individual or his ancestors. Thus were exotic metaphysical speculations tailored to suit the conceptions of conventional Greek morality" (304).

Päs, Heinrich. 2023. *The One: How an Ancient Idea Holds the Future of Physics*. New York: Basic Books.

Pausanias. 1824. *Description of Greece*. Translated by Anonymous (Thomas Taylor). London: Priestley.

> One of Taylor's clearer translations, with his usual goldmine of notes.

Penella, Robert J. 1979. "Philostratus' Letter to Julia Domna" in *Hermes* 107, pp. 161–68.

Pepper, Elizabeth, and John Wilcock. 1993. *Magical and Mystical Sites: Europe and the British Isles*. Grand Rapids, Mich.: Phanes Press.

> "The largest building in Pompeii stood at the southwest end of the forum and was a basilica dedicated to Orpheus. . . . It was at the basilica to Orpheus that the bankers and merchants of Pompeii met to discuss business. Here also judgments were made" (116).

Pickard-Cambridge, Arthur W. 1988. *The Dramatic Festivals of Athens*. Rev. ed. Oxford: Oxford University Press. First published 1968.

> Dated but nevertheless classic study of ancient drama. Useful to compare and contrast with the theatrical elements of the *Orphic Hymns*.

Pinchard, Alexis. 2012. "The Salvific Function of Memory in Archaic Poetry, in the Orphic Gold Tablets and in Plato: What Continuity, What Break?" ISNS Tenth International Conference, Cagliari.

> The abstract of this paper states: "According to this paper, the Athenian Neoplatonic idea that there was a deep accordance between Orpheus, Pythagoras and Plato about the method and the definition of soul salvation (see Syrianus) is not fully erroneous. It just has to be put in a dynamic perspective instead of a static one."

Plassmann, Joseph O. 1982. *Orpheus: Altgriechische Mysterien.* Regensburg, Germany: Diederichs. A German translation of the *Orphic Hymns.*

Polikoff, Daniel. 2020. *In the Image of Orpheus: Rilke A Soul History.* Asheville, N.C.: Chiron.

Pontiac, Ronnie. 2022. *American Metaphysical Religion: Esoteric and Mystical Traditions of the New World.* Rochester, Vt.: Inner Traditions.

Powell, Barry. 2021. *Greek Poems to the Gods: Hymns from Homer to Proclus.* Berkeley: University of California Press.

Prater, Donald. 1994. *A Ringing Glass: The Life of Rainer Maria Rilke.* Oxford: Oxford University Press.

Prumm, Karl. 1956. "Die Orphik im Spiegel der neuen Forschung." *Zeitschrift fur katologische Theologie* 78: 1–40. Survey of research on Orphism recommended by Larry Alderink who summarizes it (1981, 7ff, 134).

Raine, Kathleen. 1962. *Blake and Tradition.* Princeton, N.J.: Princeton University Press.
> Classic and important two-volume study of the influence of Thomas Taylor's brand of Neoplatonism and Orphism on the poetry of the great William Blake. A wealth of beautiful illustrations, analysis, and references.

Rappe, Sara. 2000. *Reading Neoplatonism: Non-discursive Thinking in the Texts of Plotinus, Proclus and Damascius.* Cambridge, UK: Cambridge University Press.

Reidweg, C. 1993. "Judisch-hellenistische Imitation eines orphischen Hieros Logos: Beobachtungen zu OF 245 und 247 (sog. Testament des Orpheus)" in *Classica Monacensia* 7 (Tübingen).

Roark, Randy. 2021. Personal correspondence.

Roe, Ann. 2012. *Orpheus: The Song of Life.* New York: Overlook Press.
> While her conclusions may occasionally be suspect, the information she provides and her skill as a writer make this an enjoyable survey of the prolific influence of the Orphic on Western culture.

Roggemans, Marcel. *History of Martinism and the F.U.D.O.S.I.* Morrisville, N.C.: Lulu, 2008.

Rohde, Erwin. 2006. *Psyche: The Cult of Souls and the Belief in Immortality among the Greeks.* 2 vols. Translated by W. B. Hillis. Eugene, Or.: Wipf and Stock. First published 1894.
> Classic study, by a friend of Nietzsche. "In contrast with the soul the body

could hardly help appearing as an encumbrance, an obstacle to be got rid of. The conception of an ever-threatening pollution and 'uncleanness' which was nourished by the teaching and activities of those innumerable purification-priests of whom Epimenides is known to us as the supreme master, had gradually so penetrated the whole of the official religion itself with purification ceremonies that it might very well have seemed as though in the midst of this renovation and development of a type of religious thought that had been more than half forgotten in the Homeric period, Greek religion was fast approaching the condition of Brahmanism or Zoroastrianism and becoming essentially a religion of purification—the 'soul' required to be purified from the polluting embarrassment of the body" (302).

Ronan, Stephen. 1991. "Hekate's Iynx: An Ancient Theurgical Tool." In *Alexandria: The Journal of the Western Cosmological Traditions,* vol. 1, 321–35. Edited by David Fideler. Grand Rapids: Phanes Press.
Detailed discussion of Hekate's mysterious cult object.

Rooley, Anthony. 1990. *Performance: Revealing the Orpheus Within.* Dorset: Element. Charming and inspiring application of Orphism-influenced performance theories and techniques presented by the director of the celebrated Consort of Musicke. A helpful and interesting short discussion of Orphic myth, cult, and historical influence from Ficino to Spenser and Dowland.

Rosán, Laurence Jay. 1949. *The Philosophy of Proclus: The Final Phase of Ancient Thought.* New York: Cosmos Press.

Runzi, Meilina. 2015. *Passports for the Afterlife: Orphic Totenpässe.* Athens: University of Georgia Press, 2015.

Russell, Bertrand. 1946. *History of Western Philosophy.* London: George Allen and Unwin.

Santamaría, Marco Antonio. 2014. "The Song of Orpheus in the *Argonautica* and the Theogonic Library of Apollonius." In *The Alexandrian Tradition: Interactions between Science, Religion, and Literature,* edited by Luis Arturo Guichard, Juan Luis García Alonso, and Maria Paz de Hoz, 115–40. Bern, Switzerland: Peter Lang.

———. 2016. "Did Plato Know of the Orphic God Protogonos?" In *Greek Philosophy and Mystery Cults,* edited by Maria José Martin-Velasco and Maria José Garcia Blanco, 205–31. Newcastle upon Tyne, UK: Cambridge Scholars.

———. 2016. "A Phallus Hard to Swallow: The Meaning of αἰδοῖος/ -ον in the Derveni Papyrus." *Classical Philology* 111 (2): 139–64.

———. 2017. "The Sceptre and the Sickle. The Transmission of Divine Power in the Orphic Rhapsodies." Chapter 6 in *Divine Powers in Late Antiquity,* edited by Anna Marmodoro and Irini-Fotini Viltanioti. Oxford University Press, Oxford.

———. 2019. "The Orphic Poem of the Derveni Papyrus and Hesiod's Theogony." Chapter 4 in *The Derveni Papyrus Unearthing Ancient Mysteries.* Leiden, Netherlands: Brill.

Schwebel, Leah. 2005. "Dante's Metam-Orpheus: The Unspoken Presence of Orpheus in the Divine Comedy." *McGill Journal of Classical Studies* 4: 62–72.
While Dante only refers to Orpheus once in his masterpiece, Orphic themes and echoes of Orpheus himself recur throughout the poem.

See, Truman. 2021. "Hear My Desire: Rachmaninov's Orphic Voice and Musicology's Trouble with Eurydice." *19th-Century Music* 44 (3): 187–216.

Segal, Charles. *Orpheus: The Myth of the Poet.* Baltimore, Md.: Johns Hopkins University Press, 1988.
Follows the myth of Orpheus as the essence of poetry, lingering long on Virgil, Ovid, and Rilke.

Shaw, Gregory. 2022. Podcast Episode 140: "Gregory Shaw on the Phenomenology of Iamblichean Theurgy." *The Secret History of Esotericism Podcast.*

Smith, Sir William. 1846. *Dr. Smith's Classical Dictionary.* London: John Murray.
Though dated, this three volume edition is the holy grail of classical dictionaries but the one volume "Smaller" dictionary is also useful.

Stilwell, Gary. 2005. *Afterlife: Post-Mortem Judgements in Ancient Egypt and Ancient Greece.* Bloomington, Ind.: iUniverse.
Useful analysis of specific similarities and differences, revealing the profound influence of the ancient Egyptians on the ancient Greeks, which the latter never denied.

Sword, Helen. 1989. "Orpheus and Eurydice in the Twentieth Century: Lawrence, H.D., and the Poetics of the Turn." *Twentieth Century Literature* 35: 207–28.

Tatomir, Renata. 2016. "To Cause 'to Make Divine' Through Smoke: Ancient Egyptian Incense and Perfume; An Inter- and Transdisciplinary Re-evalution of Aromatic Biotic Materials Used by the Ancient Egyptian." Academia.edu.

Taylor, Thomas, trans. 1980. *The Eleusianian and Bacchic Mysteries.* Reprint. San Diego: Wizards Bookshelf.
In this work, first published in 1790, Taylor develops a point he makes in a note to his translation of *Description of Greece* by Pausanias: "the *Orphic Hymns* which exist at present were the very hymns which were used in the

Eleusinian Mysteries." This is not the view of modern scholars. Taylor relies heavily on the Neoplatonists.

————, trans. 1981. *The Hymns of Orpheus*. Los Angeles: Philosophical Research Society. First published 1787 as *The Mystical Hymns of Orpheus*.
> Venerable but difficult, occasionally beautiful translation with invaluable notes, a long and useful introduction to the life and theology of Orpheus, and numerous quotations from Neoplatonic sources ignored by most scholars. This rhymed version of the *Orphic Hymns* is the first English translation.

Torjussen, Stian Sundell. 2008. *Metamorphoses of Myth: A Study of the Orphic Gold Tablets and the Derveni Papyrus*. Saarbrücken, Germany: VDM Verlag Dr. Müller.

————. 2011. "The Study of Orphism." *Nordlit* 9 (2): 287–305.

————. 2014. "Milk as a Symbol of Immortality in the 'Orphic' Gold Tablets from Thurii and Pelinna." *Nordlit* 33 (33): 35–46.

Tovar, Sofia Torallas. 2011. "Orphic Hymn 86 'To Dream': On Orphic Sleep and Philo" in *Tracing Orpheus Studies of Orphic Fragments*. Berlin: De Gruyter.

Trepanier, Simon. 2004. *Empedocles: An Interpretation*. London: Routledge.

Tweten, Lisa. 2008. *Evidence of Orphic Mystery Cult in Archaic Macedonian Thracian Burials*. Academia.edu.

Tyrrell, William Blake. 1984. *Amazons: A Study in Athenian Mythmaking*. Baltimore, Md.: Johns Hopkins University Press.
> Comprehensive study of the Amazon myth with focus on Athenian sexual politics and the suppression of matriarchy.

Tzifopoulos, Yannis. 2010. *"Paradise" Earned: The Bacchic-Orphic Gold Lamellae of Crete*. Cambridge, Mass.: Harvard University Press.
> In-depth study of a dozen small gold tablets found in Crete. Numerous black-and-white photographs of the tablets and the sites where they were found. Includes facsimiles of the original Greek text. "Orphic literature," he reminds us, "Pythagorean philosophy, and Dionysiac cult(s) and ritual(s) are different contexts in which the texts—may be placed—some more readily than others" (118).

Ungers, Miles J. (2008). *Magnifico: The Brilliant Life and Violent Times of Lorenzo de Medici*. New York, New York: Simon and Schuster.

Uzdavinys, Algis. 2008. "Voices of the Fire: Ancient Theurgy and Its Tools." *Eye of the Heart: A Journal of Traditional Wisdom* 1: 105–18.

———. 2010. *Philosophy and Theurgy in Late Antiquity*. San Rafael, Calif.: Sophia Perennis.

———. 2011. *Orpheus and the Roots of Platonism*. London: Matheson Trust.
Insightful scholarship includes a revealing look at ancient Egyptian influence on the ancient Greek mysteries, Plato's philosophy, up through Neoplatonism to Hermeticism.

Voegelin, Erminie W. 1947. "Three Shasta Myths, including 'Orpheus'" in *The Journal of American Folklore*, Vol. 60, No. 235 (Jan-Mar), 52–58.

Voss, Angela. 1992. "The Natural Magic of Marsilio Ficino." *Historical Dance: The Journal of the Dolmetsch Historical Dance Society* 3 (1): 25–30.
An insightful early study of Ficino by Voss. She understands the healing inherent in the *Orphic Hymns* and any ritual use of music. A must for students of ceremonial magic and theurgic ritual.

———. 1992. "Magic Astrology and Music: The Background to Marsilio Ficinos Astrological Music Therapy and His Role as a Renaissance Magus. Unpublished Doctoral thesis. City University London.

———. 2000. "Marcilio Ficino, the Second Orpheus." In *The History of Music Therapy Since Antiquity*, edited by Peregrine Horden. Farnham, UK: Ashgate.

———. 2002. "Orpheus redivivus: The Musical Magic of Marsilio Ficino." In *Marsilio Ficino: His Theology, His Philosophy, His Legacy*, edited by Michael J. B. Allen and Valery Rees, 250–65. Leiden, Netherlands: Brill.
Brilliant and essential look at Orpheus and Ficino.

———. 2007. "Father Time and Orpheus." In *The Imaginal Cosmos: Astrology, Divination and the Sacred*, edited by Angela Voss and Jean Hinson Lall. Canterbury, UK: University of Kent at Canterbury.
As always, Voss is uniquely illuminating, especially when writing about the influence of Orpheus on the father of the Renaissance, Ficino, who not only translated the hymns but performed them for his friends.

———, ed. 2006. *Marsilio Ficino*. Berkeley, Calif.: North Atlantic Books.

Warden, John, ed. 1982. *Orpheus: The Metamorphosis of a Myth*. Toronto: University of Toronto Press.
Collection of essays on the influence of Orphism on the history of Western culture. Warden's essay on Ficino is excellent.

Warren, Rosanna. 1988. "Orpheus the Painter: Apollinaire and Robert Delaunay."

Criticism: A Quarterly for Literature and the Arts, special edition: *Modern Poetry and the Visual Arts* 30 (3): 279–301.

Watmough, J. R. 1934. *Orphism.* Cambridge, UK: Cambridge University Press.
Among the most enthusiastic proponents of what might be called Orphic Christianity. "In the ancient world we have the religion of Homer, entirely concerned with sacrifice and ritual, entirely dominated by the note of 'Confiteor'— the confession of vows duly performed: and over against it the religions of 'Orpheus,' which emphasized the relation of the individual soul with God, for authority turning not to priests but scriptures. In the more modern world we have the medieval Church, a picturesque and colorful religious system based on sacerdotalism and ecclesiolatry: over against the Protestant reformers" (56).

West, Martin L. 1983. *The Orphic Poems.* Oxford: Oxford University Press.
Definitive study of the Orphic Rhapsodies, a creation myth, but not all of West's theories have been accepted by academia.

Westerink, L. G. 2009. *The Greek Commentaries on Plato's Phaedo: Damascius.* Sedbury, UK: Prometheus Trust.

———. 2009. *The Greek Commentaries on Plato's Phaedo: Olympiodorus.* Sedbury, UK: Prometheus Trust.

Zaidman, Louise Bruit, and Pauline Schmitt Pantel. 1992. *Religion in the Ancient Greek City.* Translated by Paul Cartledge. Cambridge, UK: Cambridge University Press.
Dated, but fascinating insights. "The process of degeneration reached a nadir with the murder of Dionysos and the appearance of the human race. . . . Only by abstaining from all murder, and therefore from bloody animal-sacrifice, could those mortals who opted for the Orphic way of life effect a reconciliation with the gods. This was a life synonymous with purity but it also entailed a radical separation from those Greeks who pursued the conventional civic way" (159).

Zhmud, Leonid. 1992. "Orphism and Graffiti from Olbia" in *Hermes,* Vol. 120, No. 2

———. 2012. *Pythagoras and the Early Pythagoreans.* Oxford: Oxford University Press.

———. 2020. "Orphics and Pythagoreans: Craft vs. Sect?" Academia.edu.

Index of Orphic Charms and the Sacred Songs of Orpheus

Index